It's the Economy, Stupid!

The Coming Economic Crisis

It's the Economy, Stupid!

The Coming Economic Crisis

J. L. Wertis

Published by
Bequille Publishing
Tulsa, Oklahoma

Published by *Bequille Publishing*
Tulsa, Oklahoma, 74137

Cover photo by Bradley Andrews
Unspash.com

ISBN: 978-1-7364326-9-3
FIRST EDITION

ALSO BY
J. L. WERTIS

THE LONGEST FOUR YEARS: *The Trump Administration's Assault on Democracy, and the Rise of White Nationalism*

ALTERNATE REALITY: *The Ultimate Guide to the Mad, Mad World of Conspiracy Theories*

LIES, CRIMES AND OTHER POLITICAL SKULLDUGGERY: *The Informed Voters Guide to Political Terms, Concepts, and Claims Heard on the News*

PROJECT 2025: *An Authoritarian Takeover of the United States*

MAKING GOOD TROUBLE: *A Political Action Handbook*

Available in paperback
and on Kindle at
Amazon.com

Dedicated to the Resistance

The brave and relentless fighters who stand as beacons of hope, lighting the path for future generations; the ordinary individuals across our nation who through their courage, conviction, and small acts of peaceful resistance and unwavering belief in democracy, liberty, and justice are shaping the course of history.

Table of Contents

Photo by Supradoc, *Unsplash.com*

Preface

"**It's the economy, stupid**" is a catchphrase coined by James Carville in 1992 as *"The economy, stupid."* Carville was a strategist in Bill Clinton's 1992 presidential campaign against incumbent George H. W. Bush. Then, as now, the primary concern of American voters was the state of the economy and how the economy affects their personal finances.

Trump's 2024 campaign ran on *"fixing the economy."* He somehow managed to convince his followers that the economy was bad and only he could fix it. The reality was that the economy had successfully achieved a soft landing from COVID and the GDP was right where economists see as ideal. The U.S. economy was seen as *"the envy of the world."*

Trump promised a number of things during his campaign:

"Starting on day one, we will end inflation and make America affordable again, to bring down the prices of all goods."[1]

"Under my administration, we will be slashing energy and electricity prices by half within 12 months, at a maximum 18 months. Prices will come down. You just watch: They'll come down, and they'll come down fast, not only with insurance, with everything."[2]

"Starting the day I take the oath of office, I will rapidly drive prices down and we will make America affordable again. We're going to make it affordable again. We're going to get your energy prices down by 50%."[3]

"We will bring our auto-making industry to the record levels of 37 years ago, and we'll be able to do it very quickly through tariffs and other smart use of certain things that we have that other countries don't. Energy is going to

---

[1] 8/9/2024 Trump Rally in Bozeman, MT
[2] 8/14/2024 Trump Rally in North Carolina
[3] 8/17/2024 Trump Rally in Wilkes-Barre, PA

bring us back. That means we're going down and getting gasoline below $2 a gallon, bring down the price of everything from electricity rates to groceries, airfares, and housing costs. We will eliminate regulations that drive up housing costs with the goal of cutting the cost of a new home in half. We think we can do that."[4]

"We're going to get the prices down. We have to get them down. It's too much. Groceries, cars, everything. We're going to get the prices down. While working Americans catch up, we are going to put a temporary cap on credit card interest rates at 10%. People are being made to pay 25%. Temporary ban."[5]

"Starting on day one, we will end inflation and make America affordable again. We'll do that. We've got to bring it down."[6]

Trump remarks **AFTER** he was elected:

---

[4] 9/5/2024 Trump address to Economic Club of New York
[5] 9/29/2024 Trump Rally in Erie, Pennsylvania
[6] 10/1/2024 Trump Campaign Event in Waunakee, Wisconsin

> *"We must secure our border, unleash American energy, and renew the Trump tax cuts, which were the largest in history, but we will make it even better. There will be no tax on tips. It will all be made up with tariffs, and much more, from countries that have taken advantage of the U.S. for years."*[7]

> *"I can't guarantee anything. I can't guarantee tomorrow."*[8]

> *"We're going to have prices down. I think you're going to see some pretty drastic price reductions."*[9]

* * * * *

On March 4, 2025 Trump launched his Tariff War. The S&P 500 and the Nasdaq Composite posted serious losses; and as the Dow fell nearly 700 points, 401(k)s began to shrink.

After announcing a 25% tariff on all foreign-made automobiles, Trump was asked by NBC News if he had pressured automakers to avoid

---

[7] 1/5/2025 @realDonaldTrump on X
[8] 12/12/2024 Trump 2024 Person of the Year interview with Time Magazine
[9] 1/7/2025 Press conference at Mar-a-Lago

raising prices on imported cars and parts when the tariffs go into effect:

> *"No, I never said that. <u>I couldn't care less if they raise prices,</u> because people are going to start buying American cars."*[10]

As Trump doubled down on China tariffs, U.S. stocks tumbled solidly into the red. The Dow and Nasdaq both closed at their lowest level since January 2024, with the Dow falling 320 points. The S&P 500 closed at its lowest level in nearly a year.[11]

Trump's response to the nation-wide panic over massive losses to the average citizen's 401(k) was less than comforting:

> *"BE COOL! Everything is going to work out well. The USA will be bigger and better than ever before!"*[12]

While the president has claimed that his tariffs would not negatively affect U.S. consumers, he has recently admitted that *"some pain"* is likely,

---

[10] 3/29/2025 NBC News, Kristen Welker
[11] 4/8/2025 CNN, John Towfighi
[12] 4/9/2025 @realDonaldTrump, *Truth Social*

triggering concerns about the cost of living as prices continue to rise.

Let's be real—despite Trump's promises, the average price of a dozen eggs is up 75% over last year. As consumers cope with general cost-of-living increases, they are now faced with the impact of tariffs on everyday products and on the future of their employment as the threat of an economic slowdown trends toward recession—or even a depression.

We are already witnessing layoffs due to cutbacks or company closures—and the worst hasn't even hit yet. There are people who were planning to retire in the next couple of years, but after watching their 401(k) disappear before their eyes, seeing the increase in the cost of groceries and medicines, and seeing the very real threat of cuts to Social Security, Medicaid, and Medicare, now wonder whether retirement is going to be an option for them during their lifetime.

The economy doesn't operate in a vacuum—it is a reflection of the cost of everyday goods: groceries, housing, healthcare, energy, etc.

Economic conditions should drive Federal policy, but when lawmakers manipulate the economy to favor the wealthy at the expense of the middle class there will be market chaos, business disruption, rising unemployment, and an overall economic crisis. It happened in 2007 triggering the Great Recession and before that in the Great Depression of 1929.

Because I believe knowledge is power, I wrote this book to help the average citizen better understand what is happening and the impact this administration's actions and policies will have on incomes, future retirement, and the future of our nation.

J. L. Wertis

"No matter how many toys we amass we leave them behind when we die, just as we leave a broken environment, an economy that only benefits the richest, and a legacy of empowering greed over goodness. It is now time to commit to following a new path."

~John Perkins
American Author

INTRODUCTION

Donald Trump promised to *"Make America Great Again,"* a reference to what his followers saw as *"the good old days"*—the Halcyon days of yesteryear when women were women, and men were men, and everyone knew their place. In their minds and memories, it was a time of peace and affluence, a time when we were safe and secure—sheltered from the reality of the real world. A time that only existed, for many in this country, as a Norman Rockwell photo on the cover of the *Saturday Evening Post*.

As you will see in the following chapters, not only was this a false promise, it was NEVER part of the plan. The policies and proposals in the Heritage Foundation's *Project 2025* and in Trump's manifesto *Agenda 47*, set forth a plan to destroy the very foundations of American democracy and replace it with an authoritarian oligarchy benefiting those at the top, while the average family foots the bill.

What emerged during his campaign and in *Project 2025* and *Agenda 47* were the outlines of an imperial oligarchy that would reshape America and redefine our role in the world.

Today big corporations and the ultra-wealthy are directing federal policy. Trump is linking himself to the mega-millionaires, posing as one of them while they laugh at him and take advantage of his naivety and desire to please.

It's the Economy, Stupid explains in simple language what the economy is, how it works, and how the current administration's policies will impact the "lived economy"—not the lives of the wealthy and privileged, but the goals of the average citizen—to have enough money to support a family, to save for old age, and to have security and independence. The book is divided into chapters as follows:

THE ECONOMY AND HOW IT WORKS provides a basic understanding of what drives the economy and how it affects the U.S. and the world.

KEY ECONOMIC INDICATORS defines how the economy is measured, what the indicators mean, and how they interact.

AUTHORITARIAN ECONOMICS outlines how a typical authoritarian government works, what an authoritarian economy looks like, and how America is moving in that direction.

GOP POLICIES AND THE ECONOMY reviews the policies outlined in *Project 2025*, *Agenda 47*, and those made by Executive Order, and predicts the effect they will have on the daily lives of the average American.

OUTLOOK FOR 2025-28 examines predictions made by leading economists for the U.S. economic picture if the current budget proposal and other policies from *Project 2025* and *Agenda 47* become reality.

CONCLUSION warns of how our country, our lifestyle, and our children's future will be changed if the current trend is not stopped. This chapter includes a list of things you can do now in preparation for the recession that is on the horizon to protect yourself and your family.

Disclaimer

Due to this rapidly changing political environment some of what you will read here may be out of date by the time of publication. Some new events may have already unfolded, proposed bills may have been passed, rewritten, or voted down, and major political players may have left while others may have come on the scene.

The Economy and How it Works

Trump has a number of ideas about how U.S. Government financial policies work—all of them wrong and destabilizing to the U.S. Economy. The economy functions in a predictable and knowable way. There is an order to it. There are economic laws, which are laws in the same sense as the laws of physics. There is no way to escape them. They are immutable—and they don't change regardless of how much of a fit Trump throws!

Inflation

Inflation is the overall rise in the prices of goods and services over time eroding purchasing power. When inflation runs unusually high causing prices to rise too quickly, it has a negative effect on consumers, businesses, investors, and the overall economy. Since low-income consumers spend a higher percentage of their incomes on necessities like food and energy than those with higher incomes, they have less of a cushion against inflation and are more deeply impacted by even small changes in the price of basic goods.

The most common cause of rising inflation is a rapid and unexpected drop in supply due to a disruption such as when energy prices jumped following Russia's invasion of Ukraine; or abrupt, chaotic, and precipitous price increases from tariffs.

Data released by the Bureau of Economic Analysis showed consumer spending was down in the second month of the current Trump administration, while inflation rose more than predicted and there was increased pessimism from the U.S. labor market.

The Wall Street Journal has expressed concern about the May 2025 U.S. inflation numbers reported, with some economists questioning the accuracy of the data after the federal government said staffing shortages had *"hampered their ability to conduct the monthly analysis in the usual way."* [So, they're just "winging" it??]

A botched response to sustained high inflation can end in hyperinflation.

HYPERINFLATION

Hyperinflation is a rare event, but it has happened in other countries. Once begun, hyperinflation can spiral out of control and be very difficult to stop.

Hyperinflation indicates uncontrollable price increases typically measuring more than 50% per month—especially in the cost of essential goods such as food and fuel—as demand outpaces supply. Unless something changes, the probability is high for hyperinflation by the second half of 2025 or the first quarter of 2026.

STAGFLATION

High inflation combined with high unemployment can lead to stagflation. According to economists, Trump tariffs with reciprocal levies, combined with the hundreds of thousands of government employees that are now unemployed due to Elon Musk's

Department of Government Efficiency (DOGE), is the perfect recipe for stagflation.

Stagflation is a period of high inflation, stagnant economic growth, and exceptionally high unemployment. The Trump administration's continually changing and shifting trade wars are causing deep concerns about the GDP numbers. This, combined with tens of thousands of employees across the federal government who have been put on leave or fired under the "crash and burn" initiative instituted by Elon Musk's Department of Government Efficiency (DOGE), seems to be almost a deliberate attempt to crash the economy, pushing the country into a recession.

RECESSION

A recession is a significant, deep, pervasive, and lasting downturn in the economy, traditionally measured as <u>two consecutive quarters of negative GDP (gross domestic product) growth—even if that decline is slight.</u>

Given the unpredictability of Trump's tariff policies, the pullback in consumer sentiment and spending, the unusually high and rapid rise in unemployment due to employee layoffs, and stock market uncertainty, the U.S. economy went into reverse at the start of 2025 following Trump's re-election. U.S. economic growth in the first quarter of 2025 was the the worst quarterly performance for the U.S. economy since the COVID pandemic. Real gross domestic product (GDP) decreased at an annual rate of 0.3 percent in the first quarter of 2025 (January, February, and March).

As we approach the end of the second quarter, the outlook for the U.S. economy looks even dimmer now than it did three months ago. Forecasters predict the GDP will again drop—for the second quarter in a row.

As policies like tariffs and taxes and the chaotic off-again/on-again hiring/firing of government workers in unprecedented numbers causing the unemployment rates to skyrocket, predicting the future is no more accurate than a crystal ball!

Economists measure a recession's length from the prior peak to the downturn's bottom. Signs of a downturn often are not evident when a recession first begins, so when alarm bells are clearly ringing only a few months into Trump's second term, we should pay attention. Even if the economy begins to stabilize, it can take years to return to its former level.

The longest U.S. recession ran from October 1873 to March 1879, a duration of 65 months. Since then, we have had two periods that were identified as recessions:

(1) The Great Recession of 2008-2009 began in late 2007 during the George W. Bush administration, and continued into the first year of the Obama administration extending over eighteen months. This was a period of market decline in the economy that is considered by economists as the *"most severe economic and financial meltdown since the Great Depression."* The vulnerabilities in the financial system, combined with the bursting of the housing bubble, caused housing prices to plummet and homeowners to abandon their mortgages. The value of mortgage-backed securities declined resulting in the collapse or bailout of several banks.

(2) The briefer COVID-19-related recession of 2020 officially began in the last year of the first Trump administration and continued into the first year of the Biden administration. The COVID pandemic interrupted supply chains, increased unemployment, and decreased demand for most goods and services. This brought the economy into what is noted as one of the deepest, but also the shortest, recession

in U.S. history. In the second quarter 2020 the GDP had plunged 31.4%. In February 2021, following the election, President Biden issued a series of executive actions and implemented stimulus policies that shortened the recession and boosted GDP output by 33.4%.

Each of the current Trump policies: tariffs, taxes, the DOGE dissolution of departments that support and drive the national economy, and a proposed budget that will raise the debt ceiling by $4 TRILLION over two years, and add more than $3 TRILLION to the federal deficit, are all on their own recession-triggering events!

Every indication is, that unless something drastically changes the course of events, we could be headed into a depression.

DEPRESSION

A depression is a severe and prolonged recession lasting three or more years **or a decline in GDP of at least 10% in a single year**. Current leading indicators include a sharp fall in economic growth, employment, and production following a GDP decline.

As consumer confidence declines, people become concerned about job security and pull back on spending. Businesses will have fewer customers and will no longer be expanding, building new factories, developing new products, or replacing employees that have been laid off, quit, fired or retired.

The U.S. has experienced only one depression, known as the Great Depression, which lasted from 1929 until 1941, but we may well be headed into an economy that will make the Great Depression look like good times.

KEY ECONOMIC INDICATORS

There are several measures of Economic health and stability: The Federal Reserve, Gross Domestic Product (GDP), Inflation Rate, Unemployment, Federal Deficit, National Debt, Stock and Commodities Markets, and the Consumer Price Index (CPI).

THE FEDERAL RESERVE

The Federal Reserve System (FRS) is the central bank of the United States and is seen as the most influential financial institution in the world. The FRS is composed of 12 regional Federal Reserve Banks, each responsible for a specific geographic area of the U.S.

Following a series of financial panics and a

crisis in 1907, there were calls for an institution that would prevent panics and disruptions. At the time, the U.S. was the only major financial power without a central bank.

The FRS was established through the Federal Reserve Act and signed by President Woodrow Wilson on December 23, 1913 to ensure the nation's economic stability by controlling the money supply and providing the country with a safe, flexible, and stable monetary system.

Economic historians have characterized the Great Depression as an economic disaster that the Federal Reserve System not only failed to stop but actually may have helped to cause.

The Depression began in 1929 in the United States and quickly spread around the world—the longest and deepest downturn in modern history—lasting for a decade.

At the start of the Depression, the Federal Reserve's decision-making structure was decentralized with each district governor setting policies for his district. When governors disagreed, districts often pursued independent or contradictory courses of action. The leaders of the Federal Reserve implemented policies they thought were in the public interest, but some of their decisions actually exacerbated the problem, and policies that would have helped were not adopted.

Why did the Federal Reserve fail? The Federal Reserve's leaders disagreed about the best response, and the ineffective decision-making structure made it nearly impossible for them to take effective action.

The reforms of the 1930s, '40s, and '50s turned the Federal Reserve into what it is today—a well-designed central bank with a modern framework underlying U.S. economic policy.

For over 70 years, the U.S. central bank has operated as an independent government agency. They have to make unpopular decisions that ultimately have long term benefits for the economy. The question now is whether or not it can withstand an all-out, widespread assault on their power and ultimately on the economic pillars of the U.S. financial structure.

Two months into the second Trump administration President Trump has criticized the Federal Reserve, when they decided to keep the interest rate policy unchanged.

The Federal Reserve has a dual mandate of keeping inflation low and employment high.

When the Federal Reserve institutes aggressive rate hikes, it's usually due to concern over an economic recession.

Trump has already threatened to fire Jerome Powell, the current Federal Reserve Chair who was elevated to the position by Trump himself in 2018.

Fortunately, the courts intervened. The Supreme Court ruled that the relationship between the president and the Federal Reserve is different from that of other independent agencies, declaring that Chair Jerome Powell is legally protected from being removed by the President.

However, the Fed's independence could be compromised if Trump is successful in appointing a loyalist when Powell's term ends in 2026. If so, given Trump's propensity for appointing unqualified loyalists in critical, high-level positions, our economy may be in for a bumpy ride.

If that happens, all bets are off as uncertainty clouds the economic outlook with the Trump administration's chaotic, unpredictable and economically inflationary changes in areas like trade, immigration and regulation.

GROSS DOMESTIC PRODUCT (GDP)

The most familiar measurement of economic growth is gross domestic product. GDP measures the value of goods and services produced by a country.

According to economists, the ideal average annual GDP growth should be 2% to 3% each year. A GDP that grows too fast will create a "bubble" leading to a recession when it bursts. If the economy slows down too much and too fast, it can also cause a recession. The goal is to maintain the GDP at a steady rate that can be sustained over time. The GDP growth over time is the best indicator of a nation's economic health.

Presidential policies significantly impact the GDP. Typically, the Executive Branch and Congress use GDP to prepare the federal budget, and the Federal Reserve checks it when making decisions about interest rates.

The following are factors that affect the GDP:

Human Resources: A balance of human resources is required to achieve maximum economic growth. One of the most important factors affecting the economic growth of a country is available labor. A shortage of labor, skilled or unskilled, can hamper growth. The availability of labor *matching the requirements of available jobs* is critical in achieving economic stability.

Natural Resources: Natural resources include minerals, gas, oil, forests/timber, land, air, animals, fish, birds, and water. Natural resources are positively or negatively impacted by climate and environmental conditions such as those caused by climate change. Natural disasters such as floods, fires, drought, hurricanes, earthquakes, tornadoes, extreme temperatures, etc. can have a significant impact on economic growth. The efficient use and availability of natural resources depends in large part on federal policies.

Technological Development: One of the important factors affecting the growth of an economy is the development and use of science and technology to increase productivity. If those who make the laws thwart technological growth by creating conditions or policies negatively affecting educational institutions where much of the research is conducted, a county can quickly lose economic advantage.

Capital Formation: Capital formation is the accumulation of capital goods (equipment, tools, trucks, buildings, etc.). When companies expand by investing in capital goods productivity increases and new products are developed.

Trade Wars/Tariffs: A tariff is a tax, levied on imported goods. The tariff is paid by the importer and collected at ports of entry by the U.S. Customs and Border Protection. Tariffs are typically passed on to consumers through higher prices for goods. Tariffs raise the cost of production often leading to small business failures and thwarting scientific and technological growth.

Inflation Rate: Inflation is a measure of how quickly the prices of goods and services are rising. When the rate of inflation (rise in costs) is substantially faster than the rate of income, the economy is in trouble.

While some inflation is inevitable and part of a normal economic cycle, there is an ideal rate the Federal Reserve (the U.S. central banking system in charge of managing inflation) is aiming for. **The ideal inflation rate is 2%.** A balanced approach is necessary to keep inflation in that optimum range. When inflation exceeds this figure, the Federal Reserve typically adjusts interest rates to slow down the economy for the next few months.

There are a number of causes of inflation: supply bottlenecks, shortages of key goods, tariffs, raw material costs, labor shortages, labor costs, taxes, interest rates.

Inflation can be viewed positively or negatively depending on the individual viewpoint. Those who hold tangible assets like stocks, commodities, or real estate may want to see some inflation as it raises the value of their assets which they can then sell at a higher rate.

Investors looking to protect their portfolios from inflation often invest in inflation-hedged asset classes, such as gold, commodities, and real estate investment trusts (REITs), or inflation-indexed bonds that actually profit from inflation.

THE CANTILLON EFFECT**:** The concept of "relative inflation," or a disproportionate rise in prices among different goods in an economy, is commonly known as the Cantillon Effect. The Cantillon Effect demonstrates why the Republican "trickle-down" theory of economics has never—and will never—benefit the average wage-earner. The Cantillon Effect shows the impact of inflation on financial markets and business cycles. Individuals and organizations who receive the money first (owners and developers of new, innovative products, new sources of energy or oil, gold or other valuable minerals—or recipients of massive tax cuts for the wealthy) have the opportunity to purchase goods and services at pre-inflation prices. Once the new money supply flows down to the general public, price levels increase and everyday citizens must buy goods at higher prices. The Cantillon Effect is a way for policymakers to impose a regressive tax without creating new legislation.

UNEMPLOYMENT RATE

Unemployment is a key economic indicator. According to the Federal Reserve, the natural rate of unemployment is between 4% and 5%. Full employment marks the point past which fiscal and/or monetary policy cannot reduce unemployment any further without causing inflation. High unemployment rates typically indicate an economy in crisis.

The Bureau of Labor Statistics (BLS) defines unemployed people as *"those who are jobless and have actively looked for work in the past four weeks as well as those who have been temporarily laid off from a job."*

When labor costs or labor availability becomes an issue, companies often outsource manufacturing or call centers to another country where labor is cheaper or workers are more plentiful.

Employment numbers are affected by consumer demand. As consumers buy less, company profits are less, leading companies to either close or lay off workers. Higher unemployment causes consumer demand to drop even more resulting in large-scale unemployment and a recessionary economy where there are fewer jobs than applicants.

If the situation remains unchanged, it can lead to a full-fledged depression as happened in 1929 when U.S. unemployment rose from 3.2% in 1929 to a high of 25.6% in 1933—the equivalent of 15 million people unemployed. With demand for goods falling, many firms went out of business while other companies cut costs by hiring fewer workers.

A trade war intensified the problem as countries began raising tariffs to protect domestic industries. In 1930, the U.S. passed the Smoot-Hawley Tariff Act, which placed tariffs on 20,000 imported goods, raising U.S. tariffs by an average of 16 percent. This led to retaliation as other countries put tariffs on U.S. exports causing a further decline in trade and higher unemployment.

FEDERAL DEFICIT

A deficit occurs when the federal government's spending exceeds its revenues (income). The federal government generates revenue through income taxes, excise taxes (taxes levied on specific goods or services like fuel, tobacco, and alcohol), and Social Security taxes as well as various other fees such as tariffs, an import tax paid by American companies.

The "deficit" and the "national debt" are closely related. When the country runs at a deficit (spends more than it takes in), the difference becomes part of the National Debt. In order to cover the deficit the federal government sells U.S. Treasury bonds, bills, and other securities—thus incurring a debt to the bond-holders.

The size of the national deficit is the result of budgeted spending and revenue set by Congress and the President, "ideally" based on the overall health of the economy.

When people and businesses make less money, the amount collected by the government decreases and the deficit increases. When the economy is healthy, and people and businesses are earning more, the government collects more and the deficit decreases. Ongoing deficits are the result of a mismatch between government spending and tax revenue.

The Trump Tax Cuts and Jobs Act (TCJA) of 2017 that is currently scheduled to continue in the 2025 budget proposal is anticipated to increase the deficit by a cumulative $1.9 trillion through 2028, according to Congressional Budget Office (CBO) estimates.

The Committee for a Responsible Federal Budget (CRFB) estimates that balancing the budget without tax increases on the top 10% would require approximately a 25% reduction in ALL government spending. When you exclude certain essential programs, such as Social Security, Medicare, defense, and veterans, the required cuts would amount to an impossible 85% of the rest of the federal budget!

A recent Congressional Budget Office (CBO) report warns that based on what Trump is vowing to do, *“the coming decade will be one fraught with budget challenges.”*

The last time the U.S. had a budget surplus was 2001 when President Bill Clinton had four consecutive years of surplus, from 1998 to 2001.

NATIONAL DEBT

The term "national debt" is just what it sounds like—what the federal government owes its creditors (bond holders). It consists of the sum of past annual budget deficits reduced by annual budget surpluses.

The U.S. has never defaulted on its debt—so far. In order to prevent out of control spending and default, Congress sets a debt ceiling—a restriction on how much the federal government can borrow. When Congress appropriates money to be spent, an obligation is created that the government must pay. If Congress wants to appropriate money that would exceed the existing debt ceiling limit, Congressional action is required to raise the debt ceiling to accommodate the additional spending.

Federal debt is held primarily by the American public, followed by foreign governments and U.S. banks and investors. Over the past 20 years, Japan and China have owned more U.S. Treasury securities than any other foreign nation. Japan is the number one buyer of U.S. debt. Since Japan has always been seen as a friendly nation, there has been no concern.

China is the second-largest holder of the U.S. debt. Every year since 2010, China has bought American debt, and in return, China sells America cheap goods. This has worked well for both the U.S. and China for decades. However, concern has dramatically increased that Beijing might use the U.S. debt as leverage against the United States. All told the People's Republic of China (PBOC) currently owns about $750 billion in Treasuries, and is already starting to dump these bonds as part of the trade war.

The U.S. has always been rated as stable and seen as the leading economy in the world. International investors would bet their money on U.S. debt to ensure stable returns as well as capital safety. However, the current environment of economic chaos and instability poses a very real threat of recession that could change the playing field.

Economists evaluate the nation's economic sustainability by the ratio of debt to the gross domestic product (GDP). As the GDP increases, the revenue (taxes) the government can raise to service the debt increases.

U.S. national debt totaled around $35.8 trillion as of October 2024. The budget deficit due to the proposed Trump tax cuts is estimated to increase by $488 billion annually.

STOCK AND COMMODITIES MARKETS

The stock market involves buying and selling shares of publicly traded companies. The major American stock indexes include the Dow Jones Industrial Average (DJIA), the Standard & Poor's 500 Index (S&P 500), and the Nasdaq Composite Index (NASDAQ). These indexes capture the status of the stock markets, or a sector of the markets, indicating investor confidence in the health of the overall economy.

The rise or fall of stock indexes can actually impact the GDP, as businesses adjust their spending based on the health of the stock market. Whether the stock market is a forecaster or a driver, there's a common belief among financial advisors and investors that the stock market is a leading indicator of where the economy will be in the not too distant future.

A commodity market is a financial market that trades in raw or primary products rather than manufactured products. Commodities are divided into two main types:

Hard commodities—natural resources that must be mined or extracted (such as gold, rubber, oil)

Soft commodities—agricultural products or livestock (such as corn, wheat, coffee, sugar, soybeans, and pork)

Commodity prices are thought to be a leading indicator of inflation since they respond quickly to such things as increases in demand, natural disasters, and widespread economic shocks. Long before price increases reach the consumer, inflation has already begun.

CONSUMER PRICE INDEX (CPI)

The United States BLS (Bureau of Labor Statistics) publishes an inflation measurement known as the CPI (Consumer Price Index), which tracks the cost of goods and services from month to month broken down by categories such as food, energy, and rent.

CPI tracks the cost of living by monitoring the prices of a mixture of consumer goods and services from period to period. The CPI measures how the cost of a basket of goods and services changes over time for about 93% of the U.S. population.

The CPI measures the average cost of: Food and beverages, Housing, Transportation, Apparel, Medical care, Education, Recreation, Communication, Personal goods and services (such as haircuts, funerals, tobacco products, etc). Unfortunately, the CPI cannot evaluate **WHY** the cost of a dozen eggs went up, as it did recently due to an outbreak of bird flu, or why toilet paper became so pricey during COVID. It merely reflects changes in the price at the grocery store, the barber, or the rent.

For the reasons mentioned, <u>it's not a good indicator of inflation</u> since there are any number of natural or physical disasters or other situations unique to a particular industry that drive prices up or down on various goods and services.

CONSUMER CONFIDENCE INDEX

The Consumer Confidence Index is a widely watched economic index. The CCI is a monthly survey released on the last Tuesday of every month, conducted by Nielsen, with a responding sample size of 3,000 questionnaires, that measures how consumers feel about their financial future. The CCI is widely regarded as the most credible gauge of U.S. consumer confidence.

The survey is based on the premise (accurate or not) that when consumers are optimistic, they will spend more which will stimulate the economy. On the other hand if they are pessimistic they will spend less indicating a potential economic slowdown or recession.

The survey contains five questions. Two related to present economic conditions and three to future expectations.

The most recent survey contained a special question about reasons for a decline in confidence. The two most common responses were (1) the outcome of the November election and (2) tariffs.

By mid-April 2025—less than three months into the second Trump administration—the CCI was lower than it was during the Great Recession of 2008—an indication that we may ALREADY be in the beginning stages of another recession.

The CCI is different from the monthly Right/Wrong Track polling based on 439 different polls done by various organizations. The Right/Wrong Track polling data captures the public sentiment about the country's current direction, offering insights into the desire for political change vs stability. Based on that polling, Americans are NEVER happy with the direction of the country.

In the July 2020 poll taken toward the end of the last Trump administration, 72% said the country was on the "Wrong Track." This was an indication that Voters wanted "change," and responded accordingly by electing Biden over Trump. But a poll taken 27 November 2024 following Trump's election victory for a second term, 59.9% say the country is on the wrong track.

A poll taken in mid-March 2025 indicates that there is a great deal of second-thoughts and voter remorse among long-time Trump voters.

<u>In late May the Consumer Confidence number dropped to the second lowest on record!</u>

"That's what I voted for, but this is NOT what I wanted!"

~Trump voter

AUTHORITARIAN ECONOMICS

If you are finding the Trump administration policies, Executive Orders, and mandates, exhausting, confusing, overwhelming, you are not alone—and it's not an accident. In order to fully understand what is happening in America, it's important to know the signs of a country becoming an authoritarian state—and it all starts with the economy.

An authoritarian government is one with a strong central power that lacks *meaningful* checks and balances. Such complete lack of oversight, accountability, or transparency, leads to massive corruption, bribery, self-dealing, and embezzlement.

Maintaining power and control can often

devolve into the use of strong-arm tactics, including arrest and incarceration without actual trials or hearings. Putin's Russia is a good example—or Trump's immigration tactics that are now beginning to target American citizens, legal Visa holders, and even elected officials.

Such regimes are notorious for blatant economic corruption including intervening in, or totally ignoring, legislative decisions that affect the economy. These interventions always benefit the wealthy over the wellbeing of the general public, and typically lead to economic stagnation and increased national poverty.

Lastly, authoritarian governments are prone to destroying their nation's international trade by making tariffs so high that it's impractical for businesses to continue buying from foreign companies.

The plan for transitioning the American democracy into an authoritarian state is a complicated one. It's obvious to anyone who has been paying attention that something this complex did not come from the brain of Donald Trump. So where did it come from, and who's actually pulling the strings?

Heritage Foundation

If you're wondering why this administration is so different from the first Trump administration—this isn't Trump running the country—it's the Heritage Foundation, a small, influential network of conservative and far-right groups working to tilt the U.S. toward autocracy.

The implementation of Project *2025*: across-the-board tariffs, the mass firing of tens of thousands of federal workers, attacking DEI, gutting whole agencies and departments, massive deportations, indiscriminate rollback of environmental regulations—it's all laid out in the 900+ page Heritage Foundation document entitled *Project 2025: The Mandate for Leadership.* Trump may have been elected, but he's just the "straw man." Heritage Foundation is actually running the country!

Prior to the election, *Project 2025* was getting a lot of negative attention, and by September of 2024, it was polling at just 4 percent approval.[13] Trump attempted to distance himself from it, claiming to "*know nothing about it,*" but the

---

[13] https://www.nbcnews.com/politics/2024-election/poll-project-2025-broadly-known-severely-unpopular-voters-rcna172660

reality is, the very initiative that 96% of the country disapproved of was about to get implemented.

Despite repeatedly denying any knowledge about *Project 2025* or even the Heritage Foundation, President Trump's administration employs dozens of senior officials with links to the Heritage Foundation and *Project 2025*. *Project 2025* creators are literally running the show with more than 50 high-level Trump officials plus 70% of the Cabinet having ties to Heritage Foundation.

Some of the officials actually authored parts of the proposal. Office of Management and Budget Director Russell Vought co-authored the portion that includes the drastic cuts to critical public programs, and the gutting of essential government agencies—the task delegated to Elan Musk, whose ties to the Heritage Foundation go back years.

Musk fundamentally changed the perception of what was essentially the *Project 2025* vision, albeit by another name, DOGE—Department of Government Efficiency—with the mantra of *"cutting waste, fraud, and abuse."* It didn't take long for the media coverage and public outcry to shift away from *Project 2025* and focus on

Elon Musk. His outrageous personality and unconventional behavior helped to hide the deeper goal and broader vision outlined in *Project 2025*—dismantling the U.S. government for the purpose of installing an authoritative regime.

How do we tell "what is what"? If it's policy, it's from Heritage Foundation, *Project 2025*. If it's ostentatious, flashy, and egocentric—a "vanity" project, it's Trump's *Agenda 47*.

* * * * *

Historically, when countries have attempted to consolidate economic control at the top, it has ended in corruption, inefficiency, and a failing economy. Under the Trump administration, the U.S. has all the typical indicators of top-down authoritarian leadership.

The following warning, although it was written about Russia, is applicable to what is happening with the current administration. It's a list from an article about the Russian oligarchy by Yuri Bohdanov, outlining the key reasons *"Why Russia's Collapse is Inevitable"*:[14]
(1) Centralization of power in a single person or

[14] Yuri Bohdanov, "Why Russia's Collapse is Inevitable—and What Comes Next," Euromaidan Press. 1/17/2025

a small group of elites;

(2) Dismantling of institutions;

(3) Elimination of the justice system (or use of the justice system for retribution/control);

(4) Unstable economy riddled with corruption, inefficiencies and sanctions;

(5) Use of violence for control.

Trump's Gilded Age America

The vision Trump refers to as "The Golden Age," is his vision of "The Gilded Age," a period during the late 19th and early 20th centuries when robber barons and industrialists built great fortunes while the poor just got poorer.

Trump has promised a return to the "Golden Age of America," a nostalgic and romanticized vision of the past. In all of his references, Trump is obviously talking about what is commonly known as the "Gilded Age," a period roughly between 1865 and 1902. Remembered historically as a period of rapid industrial expansion, the Gilded Age was also a time of extreme disparity between classes when powerful business tycoons amassed great fortunes while the majority of the country struggled in poverty.

It's true that from 1869 through the 1880s, the U.S. economy rose at the fastest rate in its history, with real wages, GDP, and capital formation all increasing rapidly. By the beginning of the 20th century, gross domestic product and industrial production in the U.S. led the world—but that's not the whole story.

While the overall economy was thriving, the unequal distribution of wealth remained high. The industrialists were labeled robber barons because of rampant corruption, making their fortunes at the expense of the working class. From 1860 to 1900, the wealthiest 2% of American households owned more than a third of the nation's wealth, while the top 10% owned roughly three-quarters of it. The wealthiest 1% owned 51% of all real property while the bottom 40% had no wealth at all.

Despite high voter turnout (65-80%), aggressive political campaigning, and frequently nasty elections, there were few real policy differences at the time between the Democrats and Republicans. In fact, the politicians of the Gilded Age are famous for having very few ACTUAL policies and doing very little of any consequence while in office. The reality is that business leaders spent significant amounts of bribery money ensuring that the government DID NOT regulate or control business activities.

Political corruption was rampant. Politicians padded expenses, entered into personally lucrative contracts, were partners in outright embezzlements and illegal bond issues that served the interests of the rich. In fact, political bribery was so common that in 1868 the New York state legislature actually legalized it!

One of the few subjects of contention was trade. Republicans favored high tariffs, while Democrats wanted free trade.

Trump is a big admirer of the Gilded Age president, William McKinley, and is trying to emulate him in every way. McKinley promised that high tariffs would restore prosperity. Instead it turned out to be a political and financial disaster! He raised tariff rates to nearly 50% on manufactured goods, a move that resulted in widespread Republican losses in the following election. The idea that huge tariffs are going to solve today's problem is as misguided as the McKinley tariffs were.

GOP Policies and the Economy

When Trump took office on 20 January 2025, he inherited an economy that *The Economist*, a politically independent weekly magazine, referred to in their October 19, 2024 Special Edition, as *"the envy of the world."* They concluded that *"The American economy has left other rich countries in the dust,"* citing *"an economic output that still leads the world, and a stock market that reigns supreme."*

On the campaign trail Trump falsely claimed there was raging inflation, open borders, rampant crime, attacks on our children, chaos, and instability—the exact opposite of what economists, crime statistics, and immigration numbers showed.

All during his 2024 campaign, Trump made bold promises about the economy and how he would *"make America affordable."* In spite of the numerous economic failures during his first term, the economy was reportedly the primary reason voters elected him again. Hope springs eternal!

Let's take a look at what's actually going on, including why the administration is making such seemingly bad decisions. What is the goal, and who is actually behind it all. What is the purpose of literally and figuratively crashing the American economy?

President Trump has promised to completely remake the U.S. government and wield new power as president in his second term. The ambitious promises, if enacted, would drastically transform our country, both culturally and economically, to what Russia has—a federal semi-presidential republic under an authoritarian dictatorship.

Trump is doing his best to recreate the environment that caused the Great Recession with proposals to:

(1) Reform the Federal Reserve turning power back to the banks
(2) Eliminate the Consumer Financial Protection Bureau (CFPB)
(3) Eliminate the Federal Deposit Insurance Corporation (FDIC)
(4) Return to the gold standard
(5) Impose tariffs that will cripple international trade, negatively impact GDP, crash the stock market and raise consumer prices
(6) Eliminate social programs for food and healthcare creating a crisis for millions of citizens that will bankrupt state budgets
(7) Lay off hundreds of thousands of federal workers creating a nation-wide unemployment spike

According to *Financial Report*, continuation of the current Republican policy is not sustainable, and will require a combination of spending reductions and revenue increases equaling 4.3% percent of GDP. Projections show that the budget proposal before Congress as of June 2025 will create even more of a deficit, leading to an economic crisis that will overshadow that of the Bush Great Recession!

While much of the plan was outlined in the Heritage Society's manifesto, *Project 2025,* the actual implementation goes much further and includes a plan to manipulate the dollar, the economy, the budget, and the overall Constitutional structure of the U.S. government. It's called the Mar-A-Lago Accord.

THE MAR-A-LAGO ACCORD

It's difficult to say whether President Trump is serious about every wild and crazy idea he announces, but a new one has come to light that is economically disturbing on a global level. Just what is the proposed Mar-A-Lago Accord?

A LITTLE HISTORY

In July 1944 delegates from 44 countries held the *United Nations Monetary and Financial Conference* in Bretton Woods, New Hampshire to negotiate the Bretton Woods Agreement, establishing the U.S. dollar as the world's reserve currency. Under the Bretton Woods system, gold was the basis for the U.S. dollar.

The Bretton Woods system effectively came to an end in the early 1970s when President Nixon announced that the U.S. would no longer exchange gold for U.S. currency.

Four decades later, the Plaza Accord of 1985, a joint agreement signed at Trump's Plaza Hotel in New York City, between France, West Germany, Japan, the United Kingdom, and the United States, initiated a coordinated effort to weaken the dollar against other major currencies. The U.S. Treasury Secretary James Baker attempted to address the trade imbalance by encouraging trade partners to stimulate their own economies so they can purchase more from the U.S. threatening that if these partners did not cooperate, he would allow the dollar's continued depreciation.

The plan succeeded—perhaps too well! By 1987 the nominal dollar exchange rate had fallen more than 25%.

When it appeared that the decline in the U.S. dollar was out of control, the ministers of the G7 nations gathered at the French finance ministry, inside the Louvre Palace, to hash out a plan that would stabilize international currency markets and halt further decline of the U.S. dollar. The Louvre Accord may have helped prevent a recession when it stopped the U.S. dollar from decreasing further in relation to other currencies.

Following the Louvre Accord, there have been very few interventions in the dollar's exchange rate among the G7 countries. In 2013, the G7 members agreed to refrain from foreign exchange intervention. Since then, the U.S. has demanded stronger international policies **against** currency manipulation–UNTIL NOW.

Just over a decade later, the Trump administration may be engineering the biggest shake-up in currency manipulation since the Plaza Accord—what most analysts and economists are referring to as the "Mar-A-Lago Accord."

The Mar-a-Lago Accord is quickly turning from a theoretical idea into a real-world financial experiment at the expense of the economic future of the U.S.

The idea for the Mar-a-Lago Accord, started as a theory in November 2024, when Stephen Miran, now a key Trump economic advisor, published a report arguing that the overvalued U.S. dollar was hurting manufacturing and widening trade deficits. He outlined policies to weaken the dollar, restructure debt, and shift financial burdens onto allies.

The idea gained traction in February 2025 when Jim Bianco, President and Macro Strategist at Bianco Research, broke it down as a full-scale financial realignment rather than just economic tweaks.

During an interview with hedge fund manager Erik Townsend, Bianco confirmed there is an actual plan in place to restructure the U.S. economic base, and it starts with Stephen Miran and Scott Bessent, Secretary of the Treasury. Bessent is a former hedge fund manager, Soros Fund partner, and Trump donor, who has been a big fan of these policies.

While Congress is openly discussing new ways to manage its $36 trillion debt load, the Mar-a-Lago Accord, is already being implemented in plain sight!

The proposed plan under the Mar-A-Lago Accord would involve several stages. First, the U.S. would try to force some foreign creditors, who hold large amounts of long-term Treasury notes, to trade them in for special extra-long-term Treasuries, i.e. Century Bonds.

Currently, the longest maturity for U.S. government bonds is 30 years. Century Bonds are government bonds with ultra-long maturity dates, meaning investors would sign up to loan the U.S. government money for 50 or even 100 years.

The yield on 30-year bonds right now is about as low as it's ever been, so it makes sense for the Treasury Department to see if it could lock in those rates for as long as possible.

Other countries, including Austria and Argentina, have issued some ultra-long bonds, and the U.S. Treasury Department has considered this idea in the past, but shelved the idea as "too risky."

These bonds, once issued, would not be publicly traded, meaning they would be locked away in foreign central banks, removing them from global debt markets. The benefit for the U.S. is less Treasury supply in the open market, which would push interest rates lower, easing debt pressures.

The risk is that if NATO allies get together and refuse to play along, Trump could withdraw U.S. military support or impose additional tariffs on NATO countries, creating diplomatic rifts resulting in further chaos with the stock market and the U.S. economy.

The U.S. bond market, which is worth $29 trillion, is the foundation of global finance. A consistent and stable economic environment is the fundamental pillar that supports our nation's growth and development.

In May 2025, Jamie Dimon, J.P. Morgan Chase & Co.'s chief executive, warned regulators about the bond market. *"You are going to see a crack in the bond market—It is going to happen. And you are going to panic."*

Forcing allies to absorb U.S. debt could undermine confidence in Treasuries, making foreign investors rightly question the long-term stability of the U.S. economy.

The Mar-a-Lago Accord is based on a belief that other nations will be "encouraged" to swap holdings of dollars, short-term Treasuries or even gold for long-term Century Bonds.

What would be the incentive? A combination of punitive tariffs and a threat to withdraw military protections from countries unwilling to cooperate. This is known in the Mafia world as a protection racket or "extortion" scheme.

Economic manipulation does not erase real debt, and investors may view these moves as a sign of desperation rather than strength. If foreign investors lose faith in U.S. financial stability, treasury yields could rise instead of fall, complicating the administration's goals.

The Mar-a-Lago Accord plan could turn into an economic disaster resulting in a total collapse in the U.S. dollar rather than just a weakening. We are already seeing a weakening of the dollar in the U.S. dollar index that has declined by 9% since 20 January 2025 when Trump began his second term in office.

Let's take a look at the details of this plan, how it would work, and what it would mean to the average American consumer and to the economy. The Mar-A-Lago Accord strategy starts with tariffs.

TARIFFS

A tariff is a tax on imported goods paid by the importer and collected at ports of entry by the U.S. Customs and Border Protection. The importers pass these increased costs onto consumers who end up paying more for their products. In addition, competing U.S. based companies who don't need to import parts or products will likely raise their prices to match the importer company—because they can do so and still remain competitive.

The plan is that after a series of punitive tariffs, trading partners like Europe and China will become more receptive to some manner of currency accord in exchange for a reduction in tariffs.

Why would most foreign countries agree to such a deal, considering that the U.S. fiscal situation has deteriorated significantly since the 1985 Plaza Accord? It's unlikely that the U.S. even has the bargaining power to pull that off! While access to the U.S. consumer market is important, in recent years, China and developing countries have been reducing their dependence on the U.S. and trading more with emerging markets.

This tariff policy when used as a measure to extort compliance from other countries is a double-edged sword. Higher tariffs raise costs for American businesses and consumers, potentially fueling another inflation cycle as other countries impose retaliatory tariffs. The Federal Reserve could be forced to keep interest rates higher for longer—a risk Wall Street is already starting to price in.

Tariffs in Trump's first administration resulted in a net loss of manufacturing jobs, while cutting actual investments in manufacturing. They disproportionately hurt small businesses and farmers. Roughly 30% of Nebraska farm products go to other countries that are now being targeted by the tariffs.

If inflation accelerates—as economists are predicting—the Fed would need to keep interest rates high, but that would be contrary to what Trump has clearly stated he wants.

Economists and investors are predicting a *"seismic impact"* ranging from a recession and potential stagnation to an all-out Depression due to the proposed tariff policies.

The U.S. economy is made up of a complex network of supply chains. Increased tariffs will likely lead to retaliation by other major trading powers triggering a disruption of those existing supply chains—the result of which leads to uncertainty, lower profits, increased costs, declining stock market share prices, and higher inflation.

As the world's largest importer of goods, trade policies have a significant impact on the U.S. economy and ultimately on the lives of everyday Americans. In 2023, the total value of international U.S. imports of goods and services amounted to 3.83 trillion U.S. dollars, one of the highest figures since the turn of the millennium. While this substantial number of imports helps to keep consumer costs low, Trump's threats to impose tariffs ranging from 10% to 145% on imports from other countries are creating legitimate business and consumer fears of higher prices and negative economic impacts.

Trump has repeatedly claimed that tariffs are paid by other countries. He knowingly lied to supporters at a 2024 Wisconsin campaign rally:[15]

> *"We're going to be a tariff nation. It's not going to be a cost to you. It's going to be a cost to another country. I'm not raising your taxes. I'm raising China and all of these countries in Asia and all over the world, including the European Union by the way, which is one of the most egregious, And they're going to have to pay a price now because we've been supporting them for a long time and it's no longer sustainable."*

The Trump tariff war with China during his last administration slowed U.S. economic growth and cost jobs in both the U.S. and China. In

---

[15] U.S. News, Trump rally, Mosinee, Wisconsin, September 7, 2024

retaliation China canceled a net 62,690 metric tons of U.S. soybean purchases triggering an economic crisis in farm country. When sales to China plummeted by $10.5 billion in just one year, farmers started falling behind on their loans and by 2020 farm bankruptcies were up nearly 20 percent.

In response, Trump created a new farm subsidy to farmers and ranchers to stem the financial losses. Direct farm aid climbed to an all-time high—money that was never appropriated by Congress. Instead, the funds were channeled through USDA's Commodity Credit Corporation, a Depression-era agency that can borrow from the U.S. Treasury to stabilize the farm economy—adding billions to the national debt.

The Tax Foundation calculated that the Trump administration's tariffs in 2018 and 2019 amounted to *"nearly $80 billion worth of new taxes on Americans—one of the largest tax increases in decades."*

Although the MASSIVE tariffs that were supposed to take effect at midnight on 9 April 2025 have been "paused" for 90 days, several tariffs are still in effect during the 90 day pause:

(1) A 25% tariff on all steel and aluminum imports.
(2) A pre-existing 20% tariff on all Chinese imports, plus the reciprocal rate at 125%, making the total tax on Chinese imports 145%. China has now issued their reciprocal rate for imports from the U.S. at 125%.
(3) 25% tariffs on imports not covered under the 2018 USMCA trade agreement with Canada and Mexico.
(4) USMCA covered imports from Canada and Mexico (including energy) are subject to the new 10% tariffs.
(5) 25% tariff on ALL foreign-made cars and auto parts, as well as steel and aluminum that went into effect at midnight on Thursday, April 3 (and was increased to 50% on June 1.
(6) An overall 10% tariff on ALL imported goods from any country not covered under other agreements still applies.

The 90 day pause makes the new effective date July 9, 2025.

Less than twenty-four hours after his announcement of the 90 day tariff pause, Trump back-peddled and said that “phones, computers, and chips” would be exempt from the 125% Chinese tariffs. The latest tariff announcement specified that the exclusion also includes other electronic devices and components, laptops, semiconductors, solar cells, flat panel TV displays, flash drives, memory cards and solid-state drives used for storing data. The original 20% tariff is still applicable.

On 23 May 2025 Trump threatened tariffs of 50% on the European Union (EU) *"starting on June 1."* Two days later, he extended the deadline for the 50% tariff on the European Union until July 9—the original deadline for his tariff 90 day pause.

Experts have noted that the U.S.'s overall tariff rates are already the highest since the Smoot-Hawley Tariff Act that worsened the Depression of the 1930's.

What does this mean for the average consumer? Companies that have already announced planned price increases due to tariffs include: Walmart, Lowes, Mattel, Best Buy, Nintendo, Sony, Ford, Subaru, Procter & Gamble, Stanley Black & Decker, Adidas, and popular Chinese on-line low cost fashion retailers Sheen, and Temu.

Tariffs against China, prompted Acer to announce impending price increases for its laptops, along with similar price increases from other companies expected soon on smartphones, laptops, tablets and TVs.

We are already paying more for many goods and services, and will pay significantly more once the 90 day pause is no longer in effect.

For instance, a universal tariff on goods from Canada would increase Canadian lumber prices, which would have the knock-on effect of making construction and home renovations more expensive. (So much for cutting home prices in half!)

Many U.S. companies have already announced plans to cut more than a half million jobs due to the tariffs.

A majority of Americans are bracing themselves for the proposed tariffs. According to a December 2024 poll, 74% of Americans correctly believe that the proposed tariffs will lead to higher inflation. Trump focused his presidential campaign on his "*strong economic policies,*" promising to lower prices and grow the economy. However, his proposed tariffs are GUARANTEED to raise prices on nearly everything the average family buys—food, gas, books, clothing, electronics, automobiles, appliances, wood products, etc.

The tariffs represent a blatant violation of the USMCA, a free trade agreement between the United States, Mexico, and Canada, negotiated by Trump himself during his first administration, which took effect 1 July 2020. The agreement allows many goods originating in North America to cross U.S., Mexican, and Canadian borders duty-free, lowering prices on many staple imports like food, oil and automobiles.

CANADA: The U.S. has had a strong trade relationship with Canada since the 1980s, a relationship that was re-confirmed in 2018 when Trump negotiated the USMCA that replaced NAFTA.

Premier Doug Ford, who oversees the province of Ontario, has warned they may retaliate by restricting electricity exports to New York, Michigan and Minnesota if Trump goes ahead with his plan.

Approximately 21% of U.S. imports from Canada are food products: fresh vegetables and fruit, grains, pasta, canned soup, maple syrup—and chocolate. In addition to thousands of local chocolatiers, global brands like Cadbury, Mars, and Ferrero Rocher source products from Canada. Dairy items like milk, whey protein powder, and cheese represent between 7% and 8% of U.S. imports from Canada.

Wood and textile products account for 14% of U.S. imports from Canada including timber, cork, wallpaper, carpets, yarn, fabric and printed books. A tariff on wood products will significantly impact builders and furniture manufacturers here in the U.S.—raising the price of new homes and furnishings—essentially slowing growth nation-wide and negatively impacting the GDP.

Gas prices are one of the factors that consumers use to determine "the economy." Trump's tariffs pose a significant challenge to the integrated energy market between the U.S. and Canada. Although America is the largest global producer of crude oil, the U.S. relies on Canada for more than 50% of its crude oil. This is due to the refining industry's need for heavier Canadian crude, which is less expensive. Canadian heavy crude oil is critical for U.S. refineries, particularly in the Midwest.

The proposed tariffs run counter to Trump's campaign promise to reduce gasoline prices which averaged $3 per gallon in late 2024. Energy experts warn that if Trump's proposed tariffs on Canadian imports is enacted, U.S. refineries, facing higher costs, would pass them on to consumers with prices going up as much as 30 to 75 cents per gallon.

High oil prices raise shipping costs, but also affect farming costs since oil byproducts are a significant component of fertilizer, thus raising farm production and shipping costs—increasing prices at the grocery store.

Canada is the top foreign source of steel into the U.S. According to research by Morgan Stanley the U.S. consumed about 91 million tons of steel in 2023, with imports accounting for about 27% of that total. Some steelmakers in Canada and Mexico are refusing new orders to the U.S. in anticipation of the tariffs.

MEXICO: According to Statista, the value of imports from Mexico amounts to more than $76 billion U.S. dollars.

Expect to pay more for basic "shopping cart" foodstuffs from cereals to tea. Items imported to the U.S. from Mexico affected by Trump's tariff plan include: cereal, paper products, avocados, fruits and nuts, tomatoes, onions, lettuce, cabbage, fruit juice, dairy products, eggs, honey, coffee, tea, spices, meat, fish, shellfish, sauces and seasonings, and raw sugar.

And for those who enjoy a drink before dinner, there's bad news on that front. Your Jose Cuervo and Corona will be more expensive or not available as tariffs are imposed on liquors and beers.

In 2022, Mexico exported computers ($36.8 billion), cars ($34.1 billion) and motor vehicle parts and accessories ($31.8 billion) to the U.S., all of which are targeted for tariffs.

CHINA: The U.S. tech sector will be particularly impacted by Trump's planned tariffs. China is the major source of computers, peripherals, and parts, telecommunications equipment, consumer electronics, semiconductors and integrated circuits, and medical goods.

According to Statista, in 2023, the total import value of trade goods from China to the U.S. amounted to approximately $427 billion.

A report by the Consumer Technology Association, predicts that the proposed tariffs will increase the price of laptops by 46%, of video game consoles by 40%, and of smartphones by 26%. Other tech product categories impacted include computing accessories, audio gear, batteries, TVs, and desktops.

In addition to hard goods, China is responsible for nearly 78% of U.S. vitamin imports as well as medicines for diseases including cancer and diabetes. Experts say tariffs could lead to increased prices and/or limited supply of some drugs.

According to Trading Economics and the U.S. Department of Agriculture, some common items imported to the U.S. from China that will be affected by tariffs include: Fish and crustaceans, vegetable fats and oils, vegetables (especially corn), fruit and nuts, soaps, lubricants, waxes, candles, cereal, flour, starch, wheat, milk products, coffee, tea, spices, sugar, cocoa, dairy products, eggs, honey, vinegar, apple juice, garlic.

*****

Trump has said he doesn't believe economists' predictions that his tariffs would lead to higher prices for U.S. consumers. The following organizations disagree (and these were <u>before</u> he announced the "Liberation Day" tariff plan on literally every country in the world!).

A NRF (National Retail Federation) report said:

> *"Trump tariffs as proposed, would affect prices on apparel, toys, furniture, household appliances, footwear and travel goods. On those six product categories alone, Americans' spending power could be reduced by between $46 billion and $78 billion annually."*

The **American Action Forum** estimated that Trump's proposed tariffs would raise the average household's costs by between $3,650 and $4,300 each year.

A senior economist and research director at the **Tax Foundation**, predicts that the Trump tariffs could amount to an average increase in costs of more than $6,000 per household.

The **Peterson Institute for International Economics** estimates price Increases of $2,600 or more per year for the average middle-income households.

The **Center for American Progress** predicts that a middle-income family could expect to pay $2,500 to $3,900 more each year if the tariff proposals are implemented.

According to the **Tax Policy Center**:

> *"All income groups would see declines in after-tax income as a result of Trump's tariffs, ranging from 1.7 percent to 1.9 percent."*

Alan Wm. Wolff, a former deputy director-general of the **World Trade Organization**, points out:

> *"Estimates do not take into account the fact that domestic producers will likely raise their prices if a U.S. global tariff takes effect, and it does not take into account other costs to American wage earners when foreign retaliation results in the loss of higher-paying jobs producing goods and services to sell abroad. These consequential effects substantially increase the costs to the U.S. economy."*

In the near term, these tariffs will likely result in an inflationary rise in the economy. A predicted decrease in the GDP increases the likelihood of a recession. Concern about these tariffs is making the Federal Reserve more cautious. Following the effects from Trump's "Liberation Day" tariffs, the Feds will likely hold off on any interest rate cuts until at least 2026—possibly longer.

As tariffs rise, the Consumer Price Index surges, and consumers can expect prices of goods to increase. As rising inflation reduces purchasing power, consumers will cut back on non-essentials, leading to lower spending growth in 2026.

Consumer Confidence, as measured by the University of Michigan, fell to a 28-month low in March, with people being wary about the impact of tariffs on their future economic prospects—and that was before the April "Liberation Day" debacle!

Financial markets are spooked. The S&P 500, NASDAQ, and the DOW have been bouncing up and down like a jumping jack. And bond yields have fallen. The U.S. dollar has been losing ground to major global currencies since February. Unfortunately, it's likely that retaliation by trade partners will put further strain on financial markets.

We have seen record extreme reactions in the Stock/Commodities markets and even a massive sell-off of Treasury Bonds. If this chaos continues, we will see a continuation of the current plunge in the Consumer Confidence Index.

When companies make less profit, they pay less in taxes. When the unemployment rate goes up, as it will due to layoffs and closures, individuals will pay less in taxes. The tariffs collected from companies who are still importing goods may not be enough to cover the difference, likely causing an increase in the Federal Deficit. As a result, the U.S. may need to sell more Treasury Bonds (if, by then, anyone will be willing to buy them) which will increase the National Debt ($35.8 trillion as of January 2025). The current budget before Congress will increase it even more.

The tariffs will hurt companies, workers, and consumers, leading to layoffs and forcing many small businesses to shutter. Morgan Stanley predicts a SIGNIFICANT GDP drop.

Companies will see a large portion of their profit disappear, disrupting existing supply chains and increasing production costs. Profits will be wiped out, share prices will drop, and businesses will close.

Individual 401(k)s will shrink, and there will be a significant drop in U.S. and State tax revenues stressing local and state budgets as unemployment rises, creating funding issues for basic services. As outlined, the tariffs will increase unemployment, the poverty rate, and home loan defaults—much like the Great Recession.

Trump sees the threat of tariffs as a bargaining tool to make other countries bend to his will, but so far all it seems to be doing is antagonizing our allies and incentivizing them to form other alliances. His policies will only result in a decline in U.S. production without sufficient markets to sell our goods and services.

Regarding the current tariff fiasco, David Henig, from the European Centre of International Political Economy, says there are a lot of people pushing various ideas for how the world economic system could change, but according to Mr. Henig, *"None of them...have captured the attention of President Trump. I'm not sure there's enough skill and analytical capacity in the current White House to pull this [currency accord] off. "I think you would need some nifty footwork of the likes we haven't really seen from this administration...to get to a point where countries want to do deals with you like the really sophisticated Plaza Accord. Countries around the world wouldn't agree to things that weren't in their economic interest just because the U.S. wants it."*

MILITARY SUPPORT

The concept is that the U.S. would threaten to withhold military "protections" from countries who are not willing to cooperate with the Accord plan. Trump has long criticized NATO allies for *"not contributing enough to their own defense.'*

During his speech at the World Economic Forum (WEF) in January 2025, he doubled down on those demands, stating:

> *"I'm going to ask all NATO nations to increase defense spending to 5% of GDP, which is what it should have been years ago. The United States has been paying the difference for too long."*

After watching Trump's interactions with Ukraine, Europeans no longer trust that he will come through on his promises. The countries most likely to accede to this sort of extortion arrangement are Japan, South Korea and Taiwan, all of whom currently hold a significant amount of U.S. Treasury debt and are more likely to view China as a security threat.

This time, the Trump administration is considering a financial debt swap, forcing allies to pay for U.S. defense. The idea is to force U.S.

allies to absorb portions of American debt in exchange for continued military protection.

Is the Mar-A-Lago Accord Feasible?

Regarding the overall goal of the Mar-A-Lago Accord plan, there may be some parts of Trump's actions and policies that could be interpreted as in line with the Accord, but it's unlikely there will be any kind of coordination with other countries as there was in past accords.

Controlling the level of the dollar would be a much more difficult task in the current environment. Defaulting on the U.S. Treasury debt may lead to a much weaker dollar, but there would also be some negative unanticipated consequences. If the Trump administration even begins to suggest such an idea, it would likely lead to a noticeable selloff in the U.S. bond market.

Former chief economist at the Department of Foreign Affairs and Trade, Jenny Gordon, explained that the logic was flawed for a number of reasons:

1) The U.S. would need to borrow money to reinvest in its manufacturing sector, which

would increase the value of the U.S. dollar—the opposite of what the Accord aims to do;

2) Changing consumer patterns, technology, and aging populations have done as much, if not more than global trade, to drive well-paying jobs out of America's industrial heartland.

3) Countries will move away from the U.S. dollar as the reserve currency, and Trump has said he doesn't want that.

4) Countries are not likely to want to sign up to any deal because Trump's treatment of allies will hardly provide reassurance that complying with such an accord will buy stability.

5) Lastly, even if quite a few countries did comply, it will not solve the U.S. deficit problem.

Lord Daniel Hannan, president of the Initiative for Free Trade and a member of the U.K. House of Lords, expressed his opinion of Trump's policy as *"most damaging and utterly needless. It's completely self-inflicted. If you did think that manufacturing deficits were a problem this is not how you would go about fixing it. It's not possible to simultaneously tackle the deficit problem and keep a devalued U.S. dollar as the world's currency."*

SOVEREIGN WEALTH FUND

On 3 February 2025, Trump issued Executive Order 14196—A Plan for Establishing a United States Sovereign Wealth Fund. These funds are typically associated with oil-rich nations like Norway, Saudi Arabia, and the UAE, who invest surplus revenues into global assets.

Although, Trump has signed and issued an executive order for the establishment of a U.S. Sovereign Wealth Fund, actually funding it would require an act of Congress. In any case, Trump is proceeding as if it's already a done deal.

A sovereign wealth fund (SWF) is a state-owned investment fund that manages a country's financial assets available to balance the difference between all money flowing into the country and the outflow of money to the rest of the world. It is also used to influence the foreign exchange rate of a country's currency, and to maintain confidence in financial markets. Cash reserves are held in one or more reserve currencies, mostly the U.S. dollar.

The fund is built with:

(1) Surplus revenues from commodity exports such as oil and gas

(2) Cash surpluses from tax revenue

(3) Foreign exchange reserves (also called FX reserves)
(4) Precious metals such as the U.S. gold held at Fort Knox.

The U.S., however, runs a persistent budget deficit. So where would the money to build this fund come from?

The fund invests in real and financial assets such as stocks and bonds, real estate, precious metals, or in investments such as private equity funds, hedge funds, or digital currency. The goal is to achieve long-term economic stability, reduce dependence on volatile oil or other commodity exports, and preserve wealth for future generations.

SWFs give countries a potentially bigger return than they'd get by simply holding their excess funds in government bonds. The downside is that sovereign wealth funds can be used to finance political or diplomatic priorities or to finance a war or other act of aggression against another country. As the concept is debated in various financial circles, investors and economists differ as to whether it's a good idea or a radically dangerous experiment.

We currently don't back the dollar by any reserves. We back the dollar by the full faith and credit of the U.S. government. Scott Bessent, former hedge fund manager and current U.S. Secretary of the Treasury, when asked how the SWF is going to work, said, *"we're going to monetize the assets of the United States."*

Following are some of the signs indicating that Trump is moving forward in preparing to establish a Sovereign Wealth Fund.

RETURN TO THE GOLD STANDARD

Trump is fascinated by anything gold, so it's not surprising that he is intrigued about the idea of a return to the gold standard. But could he really bring it back? Steve Bannon, Trump's former chief strategist, said he believes the President could ditch the U.S. Federal Reserve and bring back the gold standard.

The Heritage Foundation included an entire chapter on the Federal Reserve in *Project 2025* and mentioned the option of eliminating the Federal Reserve and returning to the gold standard.

The gold standard was first introduced in Germany in 1871, and by 1900 the United States along with most developed nations were using it. When World War I started, changing political alliances, higher debt and other factors led to a widespread lack of confidence in the gold standard, and it ultimately collapsed under the weight of geopolitical tensions and economic pressures. It was also one of the factors that contributed to the Great Depression of the 1930s.

Many economic experts argue that the gold standard is outdated, too rigid, and hampers the governments' ability to respond to economic downturns causing price instability. They further express concerns that because the price of gold is volatile, linking currency to a volatile asset like gold could actually introduce economic instability, and that making such drastic changes would no doubt cause instability in the financial markets and create a lack of confidence possibly leading to a full-fledged stock market crash.

There are NO countries currently using the gold standard, although most hold gold reserves in their central banks. The Federal Reserve is the central bank of the U.S., and as of November 2024 its gold reserves came to 8,133.46 metric tons.

One huge problem—the gold supply is limited. There may not be enough gold in reserves to support major economies, and there may not be enough to back the amount of currency in circulation for large economies like the U.S.

Gold and silver have surged since Trump took office for several key reasons. A major one is the impact of tariffs on imported precious metals and a massive inflow of gold and silver into the U.S. In addition, the very real threat of inflation has fueled concerns about stagflation—a scenario that has been historically bullish for precious metals.

But there's something else that could send gold prices even higher—the revaluation of America's gold reserves. In February 2025, Treasury Secretary Scott Bessent said the government could *"monetize the U.S. balance sheet for the American people. One way to do this would be to revalue America's gold reserves."*

The U.S. still prices its gold reserves at $42.22 an ounce. If revalued to the market price of around $2,900, it could create nearly $900 billion in new equity overnight. This would give the government a new pool of capital without borrowing more money or printing dollars. This could allow the government to either sell some of its gold holdings or strengthen its financial position by increasing assets relative to debt.

Revaluing America's gold reserves wouldn't substantially change anything. Although it would make the "balance sheet" look better, it wouldn't even begin to address the fiscal challenges ahead. With the national debt at $35.8 TRILLION and growing, and unfunded obligations of approximately $73.2 trillion, this measure would be a mere drop in the bucket.

DIGITAL CURRENCY

With technological advances including private-sector financial products and services, digital wallets, mobile payment apps, and new digital assets such as cryptocurrencies, the Federal Reserve and other central banks around the globe are exploring the potential benefits and risks of issuing a CBDC, central bank digital currency.

According to an April 2023 report posted on the Federal Reserve website, *"the Federal Reserve is currently engaged in a number of experiments related to digital currencies, including a* ***multi-year*** *exploratory research project conducted by the Federal Reserve Bank of Boston in collaboration with MIT's Digital*

Currency Initiative to investigate the technical feasibility of a general purpose CBDC that could be used by an economy the size of the United States."

Pete Seat, a former White House spokesman who served as deputy assistant press secretary to President George W. Bush expressed concerns about what crypto would do to America. Seat explained, *"Crypto is a scam. These investors desperately need the government to legitimize their so-called investment. Otherwise, they'll lose everything. If they get what they want, which is displacing the U.S. dollar [with crypto currency], we're no longer the reserve currency. We no longer have the power to sanction. We lose everything."*

The bigger issue is whether Trump is angling to somehow make "his" crypto coin the new fiat currency for the Sovereign Wealth Fund.

SELLING FEDERAL ASSETS

Trump wants to sell off America like it's a piece of real estate he owns. After firing the head of the organization that would typically investigate business scams, and gutting all watchdog agencies, grifters are thriving in this scam-friendly administration.

The logic is clear: the U.S. owns trillions in public buildings and land. Selling these assets to Trump cronies at fire-sale prices would add a significant amount to the Sovereign Wealth Fund coffers. The offer is *"buy a building, get special favors from the President."* From crypto to unprecedented influence peddling, this administration has encouraged and even initiated unrestrained fraud.

The Department of Government Efficiency, (DOGE) has published a list of government assets that will go up for sale, including federal land, buildings, infrastructure, and even confiscated cryptocurrency, in order to create and fund the proposed Sovereign Wealth Fund.

DOGE has already begun the process of eliminating and downsizing departments, combining them with other departments, and selling off the buildings. The plan is to dramatically reduce the size of the Federal Government through a *"reduction in the elements of the Federal bureaucracy that the President has determined are unnecessary."*[16]

---

[16] Executive Order 14217, February 19, 2025, Commencing the Reduction of the Federal Bureaucracy

Just over three months into his second term, Trump began the process of handing over major public assets to private corporations. He has made it clear that his goal in deconstructing government agencies, is to sell off government functions and facilities to corporations [especially favoring those who have made direct—or indirect—contributions to him or one of his companies, projects, or scams]. Some of the Federal Government functions being targeted are:

Prisons: Federal, state, and local governments have used private prisons for decades, until the public learned that most private prisons require 80-90% occupancy, otherwise the government would have to pay for unused beds. The Obama administration phased out private prisons after studies found more safety, sanitary, and security problems than government-run facilities. Within a month after taking office during his first term, Trump increased the budget for private prisons by $171 million.

Veterans Affairs health care: The Trump administration budget cuts benefits for disabled veterans in order to pay for a program that sends veterans to private, for-profit (often inferior—but cheaper!) hospitals and medical clinics.

Public schools: The Trump budget cuts funding for public schools transferring the money to private (Christian) religious, and for-profit schools. While public schools serve all students—rich, poor, healthy, disabled, easy to teach, special needs, etc., private schools do not.

Air traffic control: The administration has proposed privatizing the country's air traffic control. This could raise operational costs by 20-29% after 10 years, which means passengers would pay more to fly.

Roads and bridges: The administration has proposed deep cuts to existing infrastructure programs diverting tax dollars to private companies who would profit from tolls and fees from drivers using highways, bridges, and rest stops.

Public lands and national monuments: In April 2025, Trump signed an executive order directing the Dept of the Interior to review national monuments and *"suggest legislative changes or modifications,"* laying the groundwork for the removal of protections against developing and/or drilling on public lands and waters, including federal land currently designated as national parks, historical sites, and nature reserves.

Some of the groups/organizations specifically named in the Executive Order for elimination are:

THE PRESIDIO TRUST: The Presidio Trust is the federal agency responsible for the stewardship of the Presidio of San Francisco, a registered historic landmark and national park site. Created in 1996 by Congress, the Presidio Trust was charged with the task of transforming the former military post into a national park site and generating the revenue to sustain it. Since 2013, the Presidio Trust has not received any annual federal appropriations. Commercial and residential real estate leases generate the majority of revenue needed to cover the cost of the Presidio's operations. The Trust also earns additional revenue from utility charges, parking fees, and special event permit fees from a public 18-hole golf course and two hotels (that Trump has his eye on for another Trump-owned golf resort). It is an innovative financial model that is unique in the National Park system. *[NOTE: This is the ONLY organization specifically targeted under the E.O. that is NOT an independent agency. It may have been targeted because it has "investment potential" that will directly benefit Trump if it's put up for sale!]*

THE INTER-AMERICAN FOUNDATION: The Inter-American Foundation (IAF) is an independent agency of the United States government that funds community-led development in Latin America and the Caribbean. It was created through the Foreign Assistance Act of 1969 as an alternative to traditional foreign assistance.

THE U.S. AFRICAN DEVELOPMENT FOUNDATION (USADF): The U.S. African Development Foundation (USADF) is an independent U.S. government agency established by Congress in 1980 to invest directly in African grassroots enterprises and social entrepreneurs.

THE UNITED STATES INSTITUTE OF PEACE: The United States Institute of Peace (USIP) is an American independent nonprofit funded by Congress and tasked with promoting conflict resolution and prevention worldwide. It provides research, analysis, and training to individuals in diplomacy, mediation, and other peace-building measures. USIP was established in 1984 by Congress and signed into law by President Ronald Reagan. It is officially nonpartisan and independent, receiving funding only through congressional appropriation to prevent outside influence. In March 2025, DOGE entered the USIP building to replace its leadership, fire its staff, and assume building ownership. *[Some of USIP's former leadership contested the legality of these moves in court, citing the agency's independent structure. In late May, a Federal District judge struck down the DOGE takeover as "unlawful acts by illegitimately-installed leaders who lacked legal authority to take these actions, which must therefore be declared null and void." The building and other assets have been duly returned to the USIP, and all staff reinstated.]*

PROJECT 2025

Nearly everything proposed and outlined in Project 2025, from elimination of departments, functions, and agencies, to massive cuts to federal staff was assigned to the richest man in the world, Elan Musk, under a program known as the Department of Government Efficiency (DOGE).

The Department of Government Efficiency (DOGE), is a non-governmental agency run by Elan Musk, a non-governmental employee without a security clearance, with non-governmental employees, also without security clearances. It was presented to voters as a type of "audit." The so-called audit is being conducted by computer techs—individuals with no government, financial, or auditing background or training. This group is tasked with *"rooting out and cutting wasteful or fraudulent government spending"* to the tune of nearly one third of the federal budget.

DOGE is tasked with finding a way to cover the proposed tax decreases and budget increases for Trump's immigration policies, trade policies, tax cut proposals, and energy policies—in addition to his budget-busting vanity projects: "Freedom Cities," "National Garden of American Heroes," and his $45 MILLION birthday parade (not counting the cost to repair the streets from the damage caused by the tanks!).

Musk promised to *"eliminate 30% of the $6 trillion budget"* and lay off half of all federal workers. This proved to be more of a challenge than he anticipated. The fact is there are more than two million civilians working in the federal government today—70% of whom work in agencies related to national security—the Department of Veterans Affairs, the Department of Homeland Security, the Armed Services, and the Department of Justice. Such drastic cuts would not only threaten national security, but undermine Trump's *"big massive deportation program."* According to the Congressional Budget Office, pay and benefits for ALL federal workers makes up less than 4.5% of the budget. Perhaps they need to think this out again!

Even if half of all federal workers could be laid off, the unemployment rate would skyrocket overnight putting a million people out of work! That's a million workers no longer contributing to the economy, paying taxes, paying into Social Security, or buying goods, while increasing the cost to the states for unemployment insurance.

As of Musk's last day with DOGE, 30 May 2025, the DOGE program had:

Canceled hundreds of ongoing grants that funded everything from mental health programs for police officers to programs for victims of crime and sexual assault

- Laid off roughly 75% of full-time AmeriCorps employees *[In June, a judge ordered the Trump administration to reinstate grants in 24 states—additional legal action is ongoing.]*

- Removed private, sensitive personnel records and exposed agency systems to hackers and malware

- Cancelled hundreds of millions of dollars in federal grants for gun violence prevention, opioid addiction, and support for victims of violence

- Cancelled 402 grants to the U.S. National Science Foundation

- Fired more than 10,000 full-time Housing and Human Services (HHS) employees and closed half of the regional offices

- Offered HHS's 80,000 employees a $25,000 buyout for "voluntary separation" adding more than $20 million to the federal budget

- Fired all staff and closed down the Low Income Home Energy Assistance Program

- Eliminated all National Institute of Health grants that support research institutions

- Eliminated 1,300 jobs at the Centers for Disease Control and Prevention, including half of its Intelligence Service officers who serve on the front lines of public health emergency response

- Eliminated 168 Environmental Protection Administration (EPA) employees
- Cut funding for Voice of America (VOA), Radio Free Europe (RFE), National Public Radio (NPR) Public Broadcasting System (PBS). *[Legal challenges ongoing]*
- Cut all medical research grants/funding for Columbia University and the University of Pennsylvania
- Cut $2 Billion in research funding for Harvard University *[Legal challenges ongoing]*
- Cut $510 Million in research funding for Brown University
- Cut $1 Billion in research funding to Cornell University
- Cut roughly $790 Million in research funding to Northwestern University
- Cut more than 700 State Department positions and eliminated 132 State Department offices including those focused on war crimes and global conflict

- Eliminated funding for the United Nations, NATO, and other diplomatic missions
- Cut $580 Million in contracts and grants funding medical, climate, and science research
- Cut $1 Billion from USDA for school lunch programs and Food Banks
- Cut more than 70,000 jobs at the Department Of Veterans Affairs
- Stopped all CDC work with the World Health Organization (WHO)
- Cut 10,000 workers as part of a plan to dissolve the United States Postal Service board and privatize the agency *[This is unlawful. USPS is a government agency explicitly authorized in the U.S. Constitution. Legal challenges ongoing]*
- Closed dozens of Social Security Administration offices across the country
- Eliminated approximately $20 Billion in Environmental Protection Agency (EPA) funds

- Cut nearly 50,000 IRS employees **costing** the government nearly $1 trillion in lost revenue over the next decade

- Cut more than 2000 employees at the Federal Emergency Management Agency (FEMA)

- Cut Federal Emergency Management Agency (FEMA) natural disaster funds—right before hurricane season!

The DOGE plan to trim $2 Trillion from the federal budget turned out to be a major debacle with some pretty serious "OOPs" that had to be reversed—from cuts to the FAA that resulted in plane crashes, major delays, and other near disasters, and firing staff in charge of the Nuclear Weapons.

The Department of Government Efficiency has what it calls a "Wall of Receipts"—supposed savings to the federal budget. As of mid-April, according to the running tally on its website, DOGE claimed savings of $170 Billion (far less than the previously stated goal of $2 Trillion). In addition, only $70.9 Billion is itemized and there are serious doubts about that number. In fact, according to a recent estimate, the DOGE operation will actually COST the federal government an UNBUDGETED $135 Billion this fiscal year!

Nat Malkus, a senior fellow at the American Enterprise Institute has been tracking DOGE's work, and indicates they are *"over estimating contracts by a factor of two. Actual savings are more accurately estimated at $80 billion, but costs and expenses associated with staffing reductions will likely end up costing the government even more than the supposed savings."* In addition, the disruption in federal services will cost the American taxpayer in not just dollars, but personal health, financial and personal security, and overall quality of life.

A White House official confirmed that DOGE "minions" will continue to operate despite Elon Musk's departure as the agency's public face—unsupervised, unmonitored, and with no accountability to any senior official. **WHAT COULD POSSIBLY GO WRONG??**

AGENDA 47

Agenda 47, was the official outline for Trump's campaign. Although Agenda 47 and Project 2025 share many themes and policies. Agenda 47 is the Trump-created plan for policies he specifically plans to implement—many of which would be through executive orders.

The following list includes only policies not included in Project 2025 and that in some way affect the economy:

(1) FREEDOM CITIES: President Trump has announced plans to build 10 corporate dystopia cities (aka freedom cities) across the U.S. But these aren't just new urban developments. Trump's proposed Freedom Cities is a think tank known as the Freedom Cities Coalition, a group opposed to regulation. The idea is backed by some of the most high profile billionaires in the U.S, including Peter Thiel, a co-founder of PayPal, Palantir, and Founders Fund, and the first outside investor in Facebook, and Marc Andreessen, an American businessman and former software engineer. Thiel already has close ties to the Trump administration and has supported Vice President JD Vance's political career since his run for Senator in Ohio.

The cities would be pockets of deregulated areas built on empty Federal land, meaning companies within these cities would be free of typical regulations or restrictions, with the aim of promoting innovation and technological advancement. Freedom Cities would still operate within the existing framework of Federal (and probably state) power. Tax incentives would be offered to businesses and investors willing to participate.

This administration has not yet pursued the idea. It's unclear who would foot the bill for the housing and infrastructure for these "cities," and who would be responsible for potential ecological damages should these occur. As of this writing, this is an unfunded project, and it remains to be seen when, or if, the plan will get the green light, and which agencies will be responsible for bringing it to fruition.

(2) NATIONAL GARDEN OF AMERICAN HEROES, Executive Order 13978: The National Garden of American Heroes is an eccentric and expensive garden where 250 *"great figures of America's history"* will be honored through statues created specifically for the 250th anniversary of the Declaration of Independence. The Garden is set to open in July 2026, although the location of the garden has

still not been determined. The National Endowment for the Humanities and the Arts (NEH) announced they would allocate $34 million. Of that money $30 million will go to grants for the creation of statues by artists. The remaining $4 million will reportedly be allocated to administrative matters.

The project is already underway. On 24 April 2025 a press release from the NEH announced the grant program advertising *"awards of up to $200,000 per statue for the design and creation of up to three statues per recipient"* for the design and creation of statues of historical figures.

The total scheduled to be paid to the design artists is $50 Million, with only $30 Million coming from NEH. The remaining unbudgeted $20 million will apparently be paid by YOU, the taxpayer.

The Secretary of the Interior has said they will provide funding from their budget for the establishment and ongoing maintenance of the National Garden—cost TBD. It's uncertain how this will work since DOGE is continuing to cut staff and budget from the Department of the Interior.

Meanwhile millions of dollars in previously awarded federal grants intended for arts and cultural groups across the country were canceled by the Trump administration, when the Department of Government Efficiency (DOGE) cut $175 million in funding that had been appropriated by Congress. DOGE also laid off a substantial number of NEH employees.

(3) THE GREAT AMERICAN STATE FAIR: During his campaign, Trump announced that he would organize a year-long celebration to mark the 250th anniversary of the United States and host a *"great American state fair"* in Iowa.

He claimed the celebration would run Memorial Day 2025 through July 4th, 2026, and we would hold the *"Great American State Fair"* on the Iowa state fairgrounds, featuring pavilions that will *"showcase the glory of every state in the Union."*[17]

Fast forward to Memorial Day, 26 May 2025. A search for information regarding the *"spectacular event"* and it's anticipated opening leads to an announcement on the website for the Iowa State Fair: *"The Iowa State Fair will celebrate the spirit of America with our own nod to our nation's founding. Please note that the 2026 Fair—"Iowa America 250"–is NOT affiliated with a proposed Great American State Fair event, nor is the Iowa State Fair involved in planning an America 250 celebration."*[18]

(4) BABY BONUSES: In a vote on 22 May 2025, House members approved (with all Democrats voting "no") President Trump's *"big, beautiful"* tax bill that includes a new savings account for children that comes with a $1,000 deposit from the federal government—known as a *"baby bonus."*

---

[17] https://catholicvote.org/trump-announces-great-american-state-fair-celebrate-americas-250th/

[18] https://www.iowastatefair.org/visit/iowa-state-fair-americas-250-2026

It would apply to all children born between January 1, 2025, and January 1, 2029, and would be funded by the Department of the Treasury. There are no income requirements and everyone is eligible, as long as the child is a U.S. citizen and both parents have Social Security numbers.

Although birth rates fluctuate a lot from year to year, the latest number shows in 2024, 3.6 million babies were born in America. At $1,000 each, that adds up to $3.6 TRILLION dollars, at a time when the current budget shows about that same amount in deficit spending.

As of this writing, the bill is in the hands of the Senate, and from the look of it, will undergo significant cuts in order to be approved before it goes back to the House.

(5) THE AMERICAN ACADEMY: If you've been wondering what's up with President Trump attacking prestigious universities, threatening to withdraw their federal funds, confiscate their endowments, and eliminate their tax exempt status, here's the answer—another vanity project.

Trump claims that because *"the universities are turning our students into Communists and terrorists,"* he plans to *"take the billions and billions of dollars that we will collect by taxing, fining, and suing excessively large private university endowments, and we will then use that money to endow a new institution called the American Academy."*

He further claims the Academy will award the *"full and complete equivalent"* of a bachelor's degree that will be recognized by the U.S. government and all federal contractors, and will offer a *"truly world-class education available to every American, free of charge, and [we will] do it without adding a single dime to the federal debt."* His plan is to *"make the full spectrum of human knowledge available to every American citizen online for free."* [Apparently, he's remarketing the internet as a school???].

The entire proposal is predicated on revoking the non-profit status of colleges and universities and somehow CONFISCATING their private endowments. The authority to revoke a tax-exempt status from any organization lies with the

IRS, and it is illegal for the president to direct the IRS to conduct an investigation or audit. However, given that the IRS has now been staffed with Trump-appointed commissioners, all bets are off. Should he try to go forward with this, we can expect a flurry of lawsuits all the way up to the Supreme Court.

America has always been the winner in the war for talent, primarily due to our world-class universities. Attacking these Universities will only serve to force promising students to go elsewhere. There's already a global rush to recruit America's top talent to foreign universities as the Trump policies push many professionals to explore career and study plans abroad.

Successful recruitment into these prestigious colleges is what will ensure America's future with healthy demographics, a strong tax base, industry, and innovation. If Trump has his way, we will see a massive "brain drain" that will devastate the American economy in just a few short years. Canada may be the winner in this war as they step up efforts to recruit some of our most promising future doctors and scientists.

If this continues, the result will be a serious decline in the GDP and could end up with America no longer leading the world in any of the major sciences or technology.

Outlook for 2025-2028

Based on historical evidence, economists can pretty accurately predict that the current and proposed policies are likely to trigger another economic downturn equaling and likely exceeding that of the Great Recession or even the Depression of the 1930s.

The U.S. economy is projected to experience a continual deceleration given current policies and uncertainty, with real GDP growth according to the *Organization for Economic Cooperation and Development* to decelerate from 2.8% at the end of 2024 to 1.6% in 2025, and drop to 1.5% in 2026. When the GDP drops two quarters in a row, that is called a recession. Their basis for this prediction is tariffs, declining immigration, reduced federal employment, and mounting federal debt. New GDP data shows the U.S. economy declined in the first quarter of 2025 and shows no signs of changing course any time soon.

U.S. economic growth slowed sharply in the first quarter of 2025 as businesses rushed to stockpile goods ahead of President Trump's sweeping tariff policies. It's the worst quarterly performance since early 2022, when the economy was in recovery following the COVID pandemic.

There are growing concerns that Trump's wide-ranging tariffs, chaotic restructuring of Federal agencies, threats of military actions around the globe, and increasing civil unrest at home could disrupt the U.S. economy, with some economists raising the chances of the U.S. slipping into a full-blown recession before the 2026 midterms.

Signs of Economic Stress

(1) Significant negative impacts from new tariffs are driving costs up and stressing small businesses leading to layoffs and closures, and damaging trade relationships with other countries.

(2) Massive Federal layoffs due to Elan Musk's DOGE (Department of Government Efficiency) has led to higher unemployment rates and less government efficiency requiring remaining workers to be paid overtime pay. Over 260,000 federal workers have already been fired, have taken buyouts, retired early or have been earmarked for termination since Trump took office, according to a mid-April 2025 tally by Reuters.

(3) Inflation is expected to remain above the Federal Reserve's 2% target, influenced by trade policies and tariffs, potentially causing further pricing pressure for consumers.

(4) Capital markets are expected to remain cautious due to ongoing inflation concerns and elevated interest rates. Traditional financing may become more restrictive, leading companies to cancel planned expansions. The cost of capital is likely to remain high and there may be a tightening of credit terms and lending policies over all.

(5) Prices are expected to go up and household debt is projected to increase. Rising household debt may lead to reduced

consumer spending affecting businesses dependent on consumer demand.

*****

The United States had, when Trump took office on 20 January 2025, the strongest economy in the world.

We are home to less than 5% of the world's population, yet the United States accounts for approximately 25% of global economic output.

Although we are one of the most affluent nations on the planet and home to more billionaires than any other country—boasting seven of the world's 10 richest people—our general population is **not** among the richest in the world.

The term "trickle down" economics was popularized in the United States in reference to the economic policies of Ronald Reagan. The policies are based on the idea that spending by the wealthy and large corporations will "trickle down" to those less fortunate and generate stronger economic growth. Political scientists agree that the "trickle down" concept *"has been the most enduring **failed** policy idea in all of American politics...and in fact lowering taxes* *on the top 20% has been shown to actually* ***reduce*** *growth."*

A U.S. debt crisis would trigger spikes in inflation and interest rates with devastating consequences for the macro-economy. Investors would likely flee from U.S. Treasury and corporate debt, sending the economy into a deeper growth tailspin than experienced during the Great Recession.

Experts caution that addressing these problems after a crisis becomes much more costly, affecting banking and pension systems, with permanent negative effects on economic growth trajectory that will impact many generations.

America's ginormous debt poses a problem for the future of our country. The national debt just blew past $33 trillion for the first time ever, and that debt load is likely to soar even higher—potentially reaching $50 trillion within the next 10 years, according to a projection from the Congressional Budget Office. It may spell trouble ahead for the U.S., especially in the context of rising interest rates.

According to the Office of Management and Budget, it cost the U.S. $695 billion to service its debt the last fiscal year, and economists say debt servicing costs could rise dramatically in the coming years. Total interest payments could top $13 trillion over the course of the next 10 years, according to one projection from the Committee for a Responsible Federal Budget.

According to the research firm Apollo, roughly $7.6 trillion in government bonds are set to mature in the next twelve months. That's around a third of the total government bonds, or a quarter of America's entire GDP.

When the public debt balance is evaluated in relation to GDP, the debt-to-GDP ratio hovered around 97% in 2024, below the critical threshold of 100%. However, with the first quarter GDP drop and the forecasted second quarter drop to recession levels, combined with the current rate of spending and a budget that is adding even more debt, trouble is brewing. The available resources to make good on the interest of the principal payments on that debt are unlikely to be there.

Debt is not necessarily bad for the U.S. economy, any more than debt is bad for a business. The government's use of debt is a very appropriate and desirable way to finance a lot of what they do. The problem arises when the revenues are not there to service the debt.

It's certainly a problem that in the next few years, U.S. federal government debt is projected to surpass its World War II-era peak. The situation becomes a crisis when there is a sudden, large and sustained downturn in demand for Treasury securities—a situation the U.S. is facing right now. The triggers for this situation are all there:

(1) A big holder of Treasuries (like China) could abruptly start selling.

(2) The U.S. could fail to raise the debt ceiling.

(3) The Mar-A-Lago Accord could succeed in lowering the value of the dollar.

(4) The U.S. could decide to default on the payments—hurting U.S. investors who own 70% of U.S. federal debt.

In theory, it's solvable if the U.S. cuts spending and/or raises taxes closer to the Organization for Economic Co-operation and Development (OECD) average. During the previous administration, economists and analysts believed that a debt crisis was unlikely so long as the U.S. retained its strong institutions and the current fiscal trajectory. Unfortunately, what we are seeing is the opposite—a weakening of U.S. institutions and a worse fiscal trajectory.

CONSUMER PRICES

One of President Donald Trump's central campaign promises that helped him win was a promise to bring down prices on groceries.

In a post-election interview with Kristen Welker on Meet the Press, Trump declared, *"When you buy apples, when you buy bacon, when you buy eggs, they would double and triple the price over a short period of time, and I won an election based on that. We're going to bring those prices way down."*[19]

President Trump has falsely claimed that in the 90 days since he took office, grocery prices are *"going down"* and *"are down."* Grocery prices are not down nor are they going to go down. In fact, grocery prices have continued to rise, and they were up even before he imposed near-global 10% tariffs in April.

According to the latest inflation data published 10 April 2025, by the U.S. Labor Department's Bureau of Labor Statistics (BLS), the average price of food in the U.S. continues to rise.

The Consumer Price Index shows that average grocery prices were 2.41% higher in March 2025

---

[19] Kristen Welker, 8 Dec 2024, Meet the Press

than they were in March 2024. Even more concerning is that average grocery prices in March 2025 were up about 0.49% from February 2025—the highest month-to-month grocery inflation rate since the COVID crisis. This increase happened before the 10% Trump tariffs were imposed in early April—tariffs that are certain to increase grocery prices even more. The question is by how much.

Food is a major component of the Consumer Price Index (CPI). Some of the foods surveyed each month for inflation include meats, poultry, fish, eggs, cereal, bakery products, dairy, beverages, and various fruits and vegetables. Much of what Trump campaigned on was the price of eggs which hit a new high of $6.23 per dozen on average in March—about 25.7% higher than in January.

John Ross, the CEO of Chicago-headquartered IGA, predicts that shoppers will see a noticeable increase in grocery prices starting in about late June 2025 when the Trump tariffs hit every section of the grocery store—dairy, meat, produce, canned, and processed foods.

INTERNATIONAL RELATIONS

It appears that President Trump is "drunk with

power" and has decided to declare war on all of our allies. He has threatened: Canada, China, Mexico, Panama, Denmark, Gaza, Iran, Ukraine, Saudi Arabia, Jordon, Egypt, and Columbia—plus threatening *"violent and deadly"* use of U.S. military on the Mexican side of the border.

IRON DOME PROJECT: Despite military advisers stating it doesn't make sense for the United States, President Trump signed an Executive Order on 27 January 2025 directing the construction of a missile defense shield similar to Israel's Iron Dome, that he called the "Iron Dome for America" (now referred to as the "Golden Dome") to protect the U.S. from potential airborne attacks, claiming the plan would *"further the goal of peace through strength."*

Although the E.O. is posted in full on the White House *"Presidential Actions"* website, it has NOT BEEN ASSIGNED A NUMBER.

While Israel's Iron Dome is meant to take out short-range rockets and artillery fired from up to 43 miles away, the U.S. has allies north and south of the U.S. and oceans on either side. The U.S. doesn't face that kind of short-range missile threat.

Regardless, Trump ordered former Fox host and current Secretary of Defense, Pete Hegseth, to submit an implementation plan. Trump told reporters in May, *"Once fully constructed the Golden Dome will be capable of intercepting missiles even if they are launched from other sides of the world and even if they are launched from space."* He also told reporters he hoped to have it done "*before the end of my term.*"

Those who understand these things have commented *"the technology necessary to do what he is wanting doesn't exist."* They indicate that the technologies to greatly expand defense capabilities—interceptors to take out targets in space or within the boost phase of flight, along with non-kinetic options like directed energy, or lasers, and high-power microwaves would be *"many years in the development and could cost billions, if not trillions of dollars."*

The president claims *"The system would cost around $175 billion, with $25 billion to start construction in next year's budget."* CBO estimates $325 billion. Experts in the field indicate the price would actually be more in the $500 billion range and up.

Trump has overlooked a couple of key details with regard to his plans for a massive missile and air defense shield over the continent—he can't build it without Canada's cooperation. The project would need to rely on Ottawa, Canada to track Chinese and Russian missiles that could come at the U.S. from over the horizon. Right now it's doubtful if Canada trusts America enough to cooperate.

Also, given current technology, as demonstrated by the recent drone attack by Ukraine 2,500 miles into Russian territory, it would be a huge waste of time and money to develop "old style" defense systems that are useless against modern technology like drone attacks.

Trump's budget, expectations, and timeline for the project are referred to in knowledgeable circles as a *"delusional boondoggle."*

PANAMA CANAL: President Trump has threatened *"possible military action"* against Panama and is making false claims in order to justify his plan to invade and take over the Panama Canal.

Trump's repeated threats to "take back" control of the Panama Canal from what he calls excessive Chinese influence, has caused alarm in the Central American nation.

An agreement signed by Trump's defense secretary, Pete Hegseth, and President Jose Raul Mulino's administration allows U.S. military personnel to deploy to Panamanian-controlled bases along the canal for training exercises and "other activities." The deal sparked protests from Panamanians who oppose ANY infringement of their country's sovereignty.

The new U.S. ambassador to Panama, Kevin Marino Cabrer, reassured Panamanian citizens that the agreement does not permit the return of American military bases, *"Nowhere does the agreement talk about opening military bases. This agreement will strengthen our cooperation against drug trafficking and protect the canal. There is no cession of territory here."*

GAZA: On 5 February 2025 Trump said *"the U.S. will take over the Gaza Strip and we will do a job with it too. I do see a long-term ownership position"* placing the occupied territory under U.S. ownership, forcing Palestinians to leave their homeland and resettle in another country. The goal is obvious: Have U.S. taxpayers pay for cleanup and infrastructure in Gaza, and transportation for Palestinians to another country. In return, Trump would be given Oceanfront property on which he could build a Trump resort.

Just to be clear—Israel has no right to cede Palestinian territory to the United States or to anyone else. In addition, Saudi Arabia, Jordan, Egypt and Qatar, have no desire to resettle tens of thousands of traumatized Palestinians.

International law prohibits, and defines as an act of aggression, taking territory by force. The U.N. Charter says: *"All members shall refrain in their international relations from the threat or use of force against the territorial integrity or political independence of any state."*

DENMARK/GREENLAND: Trump has been talking since his first term about using military force to take over Greenland, a largely autonomous territory of Denmark in the Arctic and the world's largest island which has considerable untapped mineral wealth. Denmark, a long-time U.S. ally, has announced a new $1.5 billion military package as a step toward defending the territory should Trump attempt a hostile takeover. Germany and France have warned Trump against threatening Greenland.

IRAN: After withdrawing from the 2015 Nuclear Accord that Iran negotiated with the Obama administration, Trump has now called for a "do-over."

On 4 February 2025, just hours after announcing his plan for a *"maximum pressure campaign"* threatening economic sanctions, President Trump said he would negotiate a *"verified nuclear peace agreement"* with Iran, that prevents Tehran from acquiring an atomic weapon. No agreement is in place as of mid-June 2025.

UKRAINE: Trump promised that he would end the Russia-Ukraine war *"Before I even arrive at the Oval Office, shortly after I win the presidency, I will have the horrible war between Russia and Ukraine settled."*[20]

We are more than 100 days into Trump's second term and despite numerous efforts by members of the Trump administration to broker a peace between the two countries, attacks have continued. In fact, the Russians have not only broken numerous cease-fire agreements, but Trump is now blaming Ukraine for starting the war, while Russia and Ukraine

---

[20] Campaign rally, 26 Aug 2024, Detroit, Michigan

accuse each other of thousands of attacks that violated a one-day Easter ceasefire.

U.S. media reports claim the Trump administration is preparing to offer peace incentives to Moscow. In addition to the U.S. offering to ban Ukraine from entering NATO, Trump is reportedly in support of recognizing Russian sovereignty over Crimea, the Black Sea peninsula that Russia invaded and "annexed" in February and March of 2014 which led to the current war with Ukraine.

Negotiations between Zelensky and U.S. officials are off to a rocky start. Ukraine reportedly balked at a U.S. proposal calling for U.S. rights to half of Ukraine's rare earth minerals, about $500 billion worth, in exchange for American military support.

Trump claims the U.S. has provided close to $300 billion in support but the federal watchdog monitoring Ukraine aid reports only about $183 billion in U.S. aid obligated, with less than $90 billion actually disbursed.

Trump, frustrated at being unable to successfully broker a truce, has said he may just "walk away" from the peace talks. This is not the "art of the deal," it's the "surrender of the biggest loser."

CHINA/TAIWAN: Taiwan is facing increased military pressure from Beijing. with Chinese warplanes and warships in the waters and skies around the island. Taiwan's defense ministry said it had detected as many as 24 Chinese military aircraft along with Chinese warships around Taiwan.

The U.S. position on Taiwan remains unsettled as information on the U.S. State Department website changes daily. The U.S. Department of State's website declares continuing support for the "one China" policy while removing the phrase *"we do not support Taiwan independence."*

*****

A LITTLE HISTORY

Throughout history, there have been several successful acquisitions that gave rise to the notion that sovereignty could be acquired through negotiation for the right price. The motivations behind buying sovereignty varied depending on the historical context.

One example is the Louisiana Purchase in 1803,

when the United States acquired a vast territory, inhabited primarily by Native Americans, from France for $15 million. President Jefferson sought to secure control of the Mississippi River and access to the port of New Orleans, crucial for American trade. This purchase doubled the size of the United States.

Another significant purchase of sovereignty took place in 1867, when the United States purchased Alaska from Russia for $7.2 million. Ethnic Russians who had settled in Alaska and intermingled with the locals made up much of its population. Nearly all Russian settlers left Alaska following the purchase. The purchase of Alaska was primarily driven by the desire to exploit its abundant natural resources, such as gold and oil.

In some instances, the purchase of sovereignty was motivated by strategic considerations. For example, the United States' acquisition of the Midway Islands in the Pacific in 1867 allowed for the establishment of a naval base to protect American interests in the region.

In 1848, following the Mexican-American War, the U.S. paid $15 million through the Treaty of Guadalupe Hidalgo. Mexico ceded 529,000 square miles of land—consisting of modern day

California, Nevada, Utah, Arizona and parts of Colorado, New Mexico and Wyoming.

The U.S. paid Denmark $25 million in gold for the U.S. Virgin Islands in 1917. The purchase was considered strategic for controlling the Caribbean due to the islands' close proximity to the Panama Canal and American east coast.

So, yes, it's possible to buy sovereignty from another country, or even to take territory through war and aggression, but the price may be well beyond, in dollars and in lives, what the American people are willing to pay at a time when the U.S. struggles with debt, internal conflict, and the threat of wars around the world.

IMMIGRATION

Since taking office on 20 January 2025, President Trump has announced a flurry of immigration-related executive orders, paving the way for a widespread effort to crack down on undocumented migrants in the U.S. As his second term unfolds, expect legal, political, and economic turbulence surrounding his immigration policies.

Trump has moved to overhaul parts of the U.S. immigration system, including how migrants are arrested (without a warrant), processed (without Constitutional due process) and deported (without a hearing). Upon returning to the Oval Office in 2025, Trump effectively halted ALL asylum access.

Immigration was a focal point during the 2024 Presidential campaign. Trump vowed that during his second term, he would restrict and eliminate both lawful and unlawful immigration into the U.S. without regard to the major consequences for the nation's workforce and economy.

Trump promised to immediately deport *"the people that are criminal and have criminal records."* There are, he said, *"a lot of these people, probably two million, it could be even three million, we are getting them out of our country."*

Across the country, judges appointed by presidents of both political parties are issuing WARNINGS about what they see as an erosion of due process caused by the Trump administration's mass deportation campaign that *"could easily expand to other groups, including American citizens."*

The judges have been proven right as Trump

plans to deport LEGAL immigrants and even American citizens without due process. There is a group that appears to be on Trump's radar—quasi-legal immigrants who have been granted temporary protection by the government and are authorized to work. According to *FactCheck.org*, a Project of the Annenberg Public Policy Center, this group includes those that *"were granted protected status due to civil unrest, violence or natural disasters in their home country and Afghan allies who worked in service of the American mission; immigrants protected by the Deferred Action for Childhood Arrivals program (DACA), because they were brought to the U.S. as children; asylum applicants awaiting hearings; and immigrants from Ukraine, Cuba, Haiti, Nicaragua, and Venezuela, provided special protections."* Most of the immigrants in the Quasi-legal group are productive members of society contributing to the economy and have been in the country for years.

In early April a federal judge prevented the Trump administration from ordering hundreds of thousands of Cubans, Haitians, Nicaraguans and Venezuelans with temporary legal status to leave the country. Their permits were to be canceled April 24, 2025, sparing them until the case advances to the next phase. U.S. District

Judge Indira Talwani argued that immigrants in the program, who are here legally, now face an option of *"fleeing the country"* or staying and *"risk losing everything."*

In early May The Trump administration formally lifted a shield on deportation of roughly 80,000 Afghans who came to the U.S. after the fall of Kabul including Special Immigrant Visa holders for **those who assisted U.S. military efforts.** *[Homeland Security was being sued for its plans to end TPS for Afghans even before this announcement.]*

After Homeland Security Secretary Kristi Noem reversed Temporary Protection Status (TPS) for 350,000 Venezuelans, A lawsuit was filed in the District of San Francisco. U.S. District Judge Edward Chen ruled that the action by Noem *"threatens to inflict irreparable harm on hundreds of thousands of persons whose lives, families, and livelihoods will be severely disrupted, cost the United States billions in economic activity, and injure public health and safety in communities throughout the United States."* He further stated that the government had failed to identify any *"real countervailing harm in continuing TPS for Venezuelan beneficiaries"* and said plaintiffs will likely succeed in showing that Noem's actions *"are unauthorized by law, arbitrary and capricious, and motivated by unconstitutional animus."*

As many as six (so far) legal actions have been filed regarding Habeas Corpus and are making their way through the court system.

POSSE COMITATUS ACT: Although, on 13 March 2025 Trump announced "The Invasion of our Country is OVER," by early May he had announced his expanded use of the military in immigration enforcement through a nearly 150-year-old law known as the Posse Comitatus Act.

The Posse Comitatus Act, is an 1878 law limiting the powers of the federal government in the use of federal military personnel to enforce domestic policies within the United States. It was designed to prevent military involvement in domestic affairs without explicit authorization from Congress or the Constitution. The law reflects a long-standing American principle of keeping military power separate from civilian governance.

The law has been reaffirmed over time to prevent federal troops from assuming police functions. In *United States v. Red Feather*

(1975), the court ruled that direct participation in arrests or searches violates the Act.

In apparent violation of that Act, thousands of active-duty troops are currently deployed to the U.S.-Mexico border. Trump has designed a "work-around" that allows him to essentially violate the Constitutional intent of the law, by declaring sections of land along the border as "military installations." Among the most significant developments came when Trump designated a 170-mile stretch of federal land along the southern border—which spans through California, Arizona, and New Mexico—as a military installation, or a national defense area. On 6 May, the Department of Defense announced that a second section in Texas will be marked as a military installation.

The White House has since blatantly publicized some of these efforts and as of May 2025 thousands of active-duty troops were being deployed to the U.S.-Mexico border in violation of the Posse Comitatus Act.

Multiple legal actions have been filed and are currently making their way through the court system.

*****

Immigration boosts federal revenues, lowers the national deficit, and keeps inflation in check through participation in the country's economy, workforce, and through billions of dollars in tax contributions.

Immigrants represent roughly 21% of all workers in the food industry, 28% of all agricultural workers, and 25% of food processing workers.

As a result of Trump's immigration policies, be prepared for a major increase in the price of that steak you love. Immigrants make up nearly 40% of the meat packing industry's roughly 470,000 workers. It will not only be difficult to replace that many workers, wages will need to go up to entice employment.

Farmers will need to increase wholesale prices when they are unable to find workers to pick the fruits and vegetables. Immigrants represent 31% of crop production workers and 19% of animal production workers in this country.

Immigrants represent 17% of workers in the transportation industry, 22% of grocery and farm product wholesalers, and 16% of grocery retail workers.

According to a Brookings Institute report, removing millions of undocumented workers will have **huge economic consequences**—causing a steep rise in inflation, raising the Consumer Price Index (CPI), reducing the GDP and increasing the unemployment rate due to massive layoffs.

Economists warn that Trump immigration policies combined with tariffs will trigger supply chain issues and food cost increases far surpassing those experienced during the pandemic—only these will be permanent!

It will also cripple key industries, especially construction, agriculture, and disaster recovery.

In the construction industry, mass deportations will cause a major disruption to productivity. Worker shortages could stall projects and drive up costs. We could be faced with a housing shortage, a labor crisis for farmers, and increased property insurance rates.

Mass deportation would devastate farming operations, cutting food supply and increasing prices.

Deportations would mean fewer workers to rebuild homes, repair roads, and restore power after natural disasters, at a time when the number of natural disasters are increasing due to climate change and the government is eliminating FEMA support!

Trump has claimed he wants to deport between 15 and 20 million people (although the American Immigration Council estimates there are only 13 million undocumented immigrants in the entire U.S.). Deporting all of them would cost the government at least $315 BILLION.

These numbers do not take into account the cost of the recent and future payments to El Salvador for housing deportees. The White House disclosed that the U.S. paid around $6 MILLION to El Salvador for accepting the 238 deportees. Studies have shown that this deportation plan would add more than $1 TRILLION to the U.S. budget over a ten year period.

U.S. Immigration and Customs Enforcement (ICE) estimates a massive deportation would <u>increase the Federal deficit by an estimated $240 million</u>. This concern is echoed by the American Immigration Council stating: *"Unauthorized immigrants contribute, on average, $46.8 billion in federal taxes, with $22.6 billion going to Social Security, $5.7 billion going to Medicare and an additional*

$29.3 billion in state and local taxes every year."

The elimination of undocumented immigrants could make Medicare and Social Security unsustainable within five years, and put immigrant-dependent states into bankruptcy due to huge loses to their workforce and tax base.

SOCIAL SECURITY

Trump assured voters he would not cut a single cent from Social Security or Medicare, nor would he increase the retirement age. However, the administration, in addition to the impact of higher unemployment due to tariffs and deportation of millions of immigrants who contribute to Social Security (but never collect it), has initiated changes that could affect the program's future fiscal sustainability.

As is often the case, the devil is in the details. An analysis from the Committee for a Responsible Federal Budget found that just the Republican proposal to fully exempt taxes on Social Security benefits could drive the program's retirement and Medicare trust funds into insolvency.

TAXES

Trump has made a number of promises regarding taxes and tax cuts–most of which benefit the wealthy and corporations. Only some of them are outlined below. But these cuts are costly with no plan on how to pay for them.

"Cut the corporate tax rate to 15% from 21% for companies that make their product in America."[21]

"I will make interest on car loans fully tax-deductible."[22]

"We will have no tax on tips."[23]

"Seniors will not pay tax on social security."[24]

"Eliminate taxes on overtime pay. That gives people more of an incentive to work." [25]

"I will make the Trump tax cuts - the biggest in the history of our country – we will make them permanent tax cuts."[26]

---

[21] New York Economic Club, Sept. 5, 2024
[22] Grand Rapids, Michigan, Nov. 4, 2024
[23] Reading, Pennsylvania, Nov. 4, 2024
[24] Truth Social post, July 31, 2024
[25] Tucson, Arizona, Sept. 12, 2024
[26] Libertarian National Convention, May 25, 2024

According to the Tax Policy Center, a one percentage point tax cut across-the-board would benefit only about six out of 10 households. The biggest beneficiaries (wait for it!) would be those with the highest incomes—those making $1 million or more. Households making less than $30,000 a year would receive almost no benefit at all and may even pay more.

The 2017 Trump tax law was skewed to benefit the rich, those with incomes in the top 1%. Although Trump officials claimed the corporate tax rate cut would *"trickle down"* leading to a $4,000 boost in household income, the research tells a different story—workers who earned less than about $114,000 saw *"no change at all."*

The CBO estimates that the current tax proposals would INCREASE the Federal Deficit by $9 TRILLION over the next ten years, and boost the nation's debt by more than $5 TRILLION over the next decade.

Republicans have outlined potential federal spending cuts ranging from $2.5 trillion to $3 trillion as part of their efforts to fund a massive tax cut package for the wealthy, with dire consequences for millions of Americans.

Areas targeted for cuts include: Medicaid, SNAP, environmental protection programs, energy, Student Loan Programs, School Lunch Assistance Programs, and Federal Employee Benefits.

Areas proposed for increasing revenues include increasing fees on the shipping industry, and imposing new fees on electric vehicles, as well as imposing fees for immigration-related processes such as asylum applications, annual renewals, and visa overstays, and, of course, tariffs paid for by American companies and passed on to consumers in the form of price increases.

The current corporate tax rate proposal is to lower the federal corporate tax rate to 15%. Trump falsely claims that when he lowered it to 21% in 2018, revenues received by the government went up due to economic growth. Economists tell a different story. While there was some economic growth, it did not cover the loss in tax revenue. In fact, the previous Trump corporate tax cut ADDED $2.5 BILLION TO THE NATIONAL DEBT. The proposed tax changes are a recipe for an economic collapse of epic proportions.

It's basic **ECONOMICS 101**: The average family

will have significantly less money and will buy less—which means companies will sell less—which means layoffs—which means more people will be unemployed and have less money to spend—causing companies to go out of business—creating a huge Federal budget deficit. The definition of a Depression: A DRAMATIC AND SUSTAINED DOWNTURN IN ECONOMIC ACTIVITY, WITH SYMPTOMS INCLUDING A SHARP FALL IN ECONOMIC GROWTH (GDP), EMPLOYMENT, AND PRODUCTION.

BUDGET DEFICIT/DEBT

In the first half of 2025, the U.S. budget deficit has grown to more than $1.3 TRILLION—the second highest six-month deficit on record! In CBO's future projections, the federal budget deficit for fiscal year 2025 will top $1.9 Trillion.

House Republicans narrowly approved their proposed budget framework in early April containing $4.5 trillion in tax cuts primarily benefiting the top 10%, and $1.5 trillion in cuts to federal programs and services.

Maya MacGuineas, president of the nonpartisan Committee for a Responsible Federal Budget, expressed concern, *"The numbers are undeniable. We are racking up debt at an alarming pace, and it's unlikely to end any time soon. In fact, lawmakers seem hell-bent on adding to that sum with trillions of unpaid-for tax cuts and spending increases. We need to correct the unsustainable course we are on and start focusing on fixing our nation's finances before it is too late."*

Treasury Secretary Scott Bessent warns *"We are going to go onto the warning track sometime in May or June."*

Conclusion

Regardless of what happens in the mid-terms or even the next presidential election, we are in serious trouble. It will take years—perhaps a decade or more to undo the damage that has already been done, plus what is still to come.

From the disastrous bulldozing of federal departments, agencies, and protocols; to the appointment of the most corrupt, unqualified, and unethical cabinet members in history; to the insane on-again, off-again tariff trade policies—it's a really frightening time. If you're feeling like the future looks pretty grim, your concerns are justified.

The United States is being dismantled—from our foreign policy, to our economy, to our democracy. President Trump's policies and actions are challenging the very foundations of the constitutional democracy upon which America was built and has stood for 250 years.

History shows that no empire lasts forever. Empires rise and fall, but typically a decline such as we're experiencing is due to external forces and takes place over a long period of time. They rarely self-destruct as quickly and dramatically as the U.S. is doing under Trump.

In his first 100 days, Trump has destroyed the United States' position on the world stage—taking it from a global power to an international pariah. Despite whatever military and economic power the U.S. still has, the global image and leadership of America has been undermined by President Trump's foreign policy decisions, provoking friends and foes alike.

Besides his chaotic tariff policies that have destabilized the stock market, the U.S. Treasuries, and threatened the value of the American dollar, his proposals for territorial expansion into Greenland, Panama, Canada, and Gaza has turned the global view of America from ally to threat. His lust for power has overtones of Nazi Germany imperialism—driven and supported by an administration staffed with known Nazi sympathizers who have his ear.

Trump's insistence that the U.S. will take control of Gaza, evicting almost two million people from their homeland in order to create a "Mar-A-Lago Riviera Resort" has resulted in international condemnation, correctly labeling it *"an international crime that amounts to ethnic cleansing."*

Even if Trump and the Republican Party were to somehow lose power, the damage that has been done, economically, globally, and politically, is not easily or quickly undone.

What Should We Expect?

There is no way to stop what is already happening. Due to tariffs already in place, prices of groceries, gas, lumber, cars, toys, clothing, etc. will increase—and once they increase, even if tariffs are later lowered or removed, it's unlikely prices will come back down any time soon.

The stock market may recover temporarily, but companies have already made decisions that will affect U.S. commerce for the next decade as expansions are cancelled, people are laid off, small businesses close, and farmers go bankrupt from lack of labor, fertilizer, and foreign markets for their crops.

Betting markets are putting the odds at 64% that we are headed for a SEVERE GLOBAL RECESSION—an extended period of economic decline around the world. Such a situation is created when trade relations and international financial systems fall like dominoes, transmitting economic shocks and recessionary impact from one country to another.

Currently, the bond market is in chaos, and we are already seeing hedge funds repositioning with large sell offs. It would not be surprising to see some parts of financial markets start to break, as large institutional investors back out. The only certainty is extreme volatility in the market for the foreseeable future.

On 15 May 2025, Moody's Rating Service downgraded the U.S. credit rating for the first time in more than 100 years noting *"the U.S. debt to GDP ratio is on track to hit 134% by 2035."* Moody's further expressed concern, *"We expect federal deficits to widen, reaching nearly 9% of GDP by 2035, up from 6.4% in 2024, driven mainly by increased interest payments on debt, rising entitlement spending, and relatively low revenue generation."* They further noted *"federal interest payments are set to equal ~30% of revenue by 2035, and deficit spending is currently at WWII levels as a percentage of GDP."*

From a macroeconomic view, we should expect higher inflation, slower economic growth, and general uncertainty regarding Federal interest rates.

The housing market is likely to be unstable, with mortgage defaults due to nationwide unemployment, volatile mortgage rates, and the rising cost of new homes due to tariffs on building materials.

Our national debt is predicted to be heading for a crisis as foreign buyers abandon U.S. Treasury bonds due to the fiscal instability of the U.S. dollar and the stock market.

Then there's the threat of a war. With Trump threatening to invade sovereign nations, he may just trigger an actual situation that will require "boots on the ground." Or, God forbid, he may in a fit of pique decide to deploy nuclear weapons against countries that displease him.

*****

If Donald Trump completes his second term, he will set the record as the oldest president in U.S. history, as experts express concerns about his mental health and his ability to make rational decisions during very challenging times. We have a commander in chief who apparently spends most of his time glued to his cellphone in what can only be described as a whirlwind of apparent senility with increasingly bizarre outbursts and declarations. Even former Trump confidants are noticing that *"he has grown increasingly incoherent and rambling."* They further noted that he shows signs of awareness about his cognitive decline, and tries to cover it up with convoluted explanations, like claiming it's *"something called the weave."*

PREPARING FOR A RECESSION

Perhaps much of what Trump says is just bluster or placating his followers. Perhaps the Republicans in Congress will take back their congressionally-defined power and stand up to him. Unfortunately, right now that looks pretty unlikely.

On the positive side, so far the Judiciary Branch of the government is holding, stopping many of his more unhinged, or unconstitutional policies, but they certainly have their work cut out for them. It's uncertain how long they can stand.

Whatever is ahead, it's important to be prepared for the worst even while hoping for the best. Whatever the situation, the following list is a summary of advice from various finance experts:

1. CREATE A BUDGET

If you don't already have one, creating a budget can give you a better handle on how much it costs to maintain your current standard of living so you can make the best decisions about what you may need to "temporarily" eliminate and what changes may need to be made.

2. GET DEBT UNDER CONTROL

If your budget shows that you're spending a large part of your income on credit card and loan payments, that leaves little to protect you against an unpredictable economic situation.

If paying off your debts isn't a possibility, consolidating debt to a fixed rate loan may save money on interest and create predictable monthly payments.

3. CREATE AN EMERGENCY FUND

Recessions and job losses generally go together, so now is the time to put a plan in place should you lose your income. One way to shore up your cash reserves is to temporarily cut back on the amount of your 401(k) contributions in order to build up an emergency fund of cash that will be readily available should you need it. When things get better, if you want, you can contribute extra to catch up. Having a bit of cash reserve can help ease you through a new job search period should it be necessary.

4. Pare Down Expenses

There are many ways to save money without seriously affecting your lifestyle. Look at your budget and see if you are paying for subscriptions and/or services that you can do without or cut back on.

5. Rethink Big Purchases

Before you make a commitment like buying a new car, or boat, or decide to take that luxury vacation or cruise, you may want to reconsider and put that extra cash into your emergency fund.

6. Limit Meals Out to Special Occasions

Food is often one of the largest discretionary expenses in any household budget. Eating at home can be cheaper than takeout or restaurant dining, and could save you hundreds, if not thousands of dollars during a recession. You might even eat healthier.

7. Move Your Savings

A recession such as what we're looking at now means a declining stock market, so you need to be smart about where you put your money over the next few years.

Setting up your Emergency Fund in a Money Market Account with your bank or credit union, can earn you decent interest, but you'll also have access to it (without penalty) should you need it. This is where you would put at least part of the money you are currently contributing to your 401(k).

Although in a recession interest rates may go down, MMAs will still offer higher interest rates than standard savings or checking accounts. Many MMAs employ tiered interest rates, so the higher your balance, the higher the dividends you are paid. This tiered structure means that your money works harder for you—the more you save, the more you earn, which creates a cycle of financial growth.

Some MMAs also allow the compounding of dividends, which can substantially boost your total returns over time. This means the interest earned on your account gets added to your original investment, which then makes even more interest. Over time, the power of compounding can significantly increase your savings.

Banking your savings in a Money Market Account may not give you the return you could get in the stock market—but you won't risk losing your initial investment either! Check with the financial institution about withdrawal restrictions.

8. Convert Retirement Funds to Roth Accounts

In the event you're laid off or have your hours reduced, this may be a good time to reorganize your retirement savings. Low-income years are the perfect time to complete a Roth conversion where your money will grow tax-free.

Moving money from a traditional IRA or 401(k) account to a Roth account means you'll have to pay regular income tax on the amount converted. A low-income year could mean you'll pay those taxes in a lower bracket.

9. Stay the Course With Investments

<u>The worst thing you can do is pull money out of the market during a downturn.</u> If you cash out investments during a stock market correction—and we certainly have some pretty wild swings these days—you could miss the rebound. In fact,

some of the best trading days in the market happen right after the worst days. Unless you really need the money within the next 3-4 years, stay the course.

10. DELAY YOUR RETIREMENT

If you were planning to retire within the next four years, it may be better to wait until the economy rebounds. Retiring in a down market can be difficult. Dipping into your retirement funds to pay bills and making early retirement withdrawals could leave you without enough cash later on.

11. TAKE SOCIAL SECURITY EARLY

If you're at least age 62 and lose your job, you may want to consider starting your Social Security benefits early. Taking Social Security early means you'll receive a reduced benefit if you start your claim before full retirement age—currently age 67.

Before you make that decision, be sure you can live on the reduced income (See #1—Create a Budget). Will Social Security be enough to cover essential bills? If not, do you have other sources of income that can make up the difference? In doing that calculation, keep in mind that during a recession (especially THIS ONE) prices are likely to significantly increase from what they are now for basic necessities: groceries, medical bills and medications, housing, insurance, etc.

Medicare is not available until age 65, so don't forget to calculate the cost of medical insurance and prescription drugs which you may be getting now through your employee health plan. Check costs online for coverage under the Affordable Care Act (ACA).

Unfortunately, Medicaid is not likely to be an alternative option since it's currently under threat and may be cut or seriously limited by the time you read this.

12. CONSIDER DOWNSIZING

Your house and mortgage are likely your biggest expenses. If you lose your job, downsizing may be your best option.

If your home is paid in full or you have significant equity, selling may provide additional funds for living expenses, even considering the costs associated with selling a home and buying a cheaper one.

You may want to consider moving to a small town where homes and/or rent is less expensive. Also, during a recession crime tends to go up, and small towns are generally safer.

13. Reduce Your Energy Costs

If you think you'll have trouble covering your energy costs during a recession, research what assistance is available. Utility companies and nonprofit organizations may have programs available to reduce costs for those who are income eligible. Unfortunately, the Federal Energy Assistance program has been eliminated by DOGE.

14. Verify Your Insurance Coverage

Getting sick can mean lost income and high medical bills. Take advantage of your open enrollment period to review your health insurance coverage and make changes as necessary.

15. Shop for Values and Bargains

Get your produce from farm stalls or farmer's markets. It's not only fresher, but it will help the farmers who may be struggling.

Make shopping a treasure hunt by shopping at thrift stores, garage sales, swap meets and flea markets. It can be a fun family outing and help with the budget.

FYI, thrift store shopping is "in" again with the younger crowd!

Final Thoughts

During these difficult times, it's easy to feel overwhelmed and discouraged. The continued uncertainty is a heavy burden and can make it seem as though things will never improve. Those who came before us must have felt the same emotions we are feeling now, yet they persevered.

Sometimes opportunity comes disguised as adversity. With the right mindset, we can not only endure difficulties but also grow through a shift in perspective. History shows that individuals often emerge from difficult experiences with a deeper sense of purpose, greater appreciation for life, and increased emotional strength. Hardships challenge us to find new coping strategies and provide the time and space to reassess our priorities. Difficulties can become catalysts for transformation rather than mere obstacles to endure.

No leader, king, demagogue, dictator or president rules forever. No amount of power, money, or popularity can stop the inevitable. Some will be voted out of office, impeached, or will voluntarily resign. Some will die in office from natural causes, suicide, assassination, or accident. Whatever the situation, all are eventually removed from power. When that happens there is an opportunity for the country to re-assess values, rebuild the political structure, implement stronger guardrails, and plot a new course.

This administration has already done permanent damage to the American economy. Congress has ceded their Constitutional duties to a President who has used them to violate the laws of the land and the Constitution itself for the enrichment of the wealthy at the price of the health and wellbeing of the citizens.

It is two and a half centuries since the Founding Fathers commenced what they knew to be a bold test of democracy, freedom, and progress known as the "American Experiment." If this administration is allowed to continue on the current path of total destruction of both the economy and America's standing in the world, that will be the end of American democracy as we know it.

But there is hope! EVERY authoritarian, totalitarian and fascist regime in history eventually failed, thanks to the PEOPLE.

Our task as citizens is to identify capable, bright, and honest persons and vote them into leadership to replace the incompetent, self-serving, malicious, callous ones now in Congress and the White House.

> *To be hopeful in bad times is based on the fact that human history is not only of cruelty, but also of compassion, sacrifice, courage, kindness. If we see only the worst, it destroys our capacity to do something. If we remember those times and places where people have behaved magnificently, this gives us the energy to act. And if we do act, in however small a way, we don't have to wait for some grand Utopian future. The future is an infinite succession of presents, and to live now as we think human beings should live, in defiance of all that is bad around us, is itself a marvelous victory.*
>
> *~Howard Zinn, Historian*

About the Author

J. L. Wertis is a non-fiction author who writes in the genres of politics, theology, philosophy, and family history/genealogy.

Ms. Wertis did her undergraduate studies in social psychology and has a Bachelor of Science in Computer Information Systems, a Master's in Business Administration-Finance, and did post graduate work (just short of a PhD) in Business Economics-Law.

She had a long career as a financial manager in city and county government and in federally funded agencies.

Throughout the years she has maintained an active interest in social psychology, studying how social and political influences affect individual and group behavior. This interest adds depth to her political, genealogical, and philosophical works.

She is a member of PEN America, a nonprofit that defends the right to expression through the written word.

Made in the USA
Monee, IL
04 November 2026

67380406R00095